A bit of fun for you,
Fran. love Chrissie xx
may, 2021

Old Seems
to be
Other People

Lily Brett was born in Germany and came to Melbourne with her parents in 1948. She is one of Australia's most loved, prolific and successful authors. She has published six works of fiction, nine books of poetry and four essay collections, to much critical acclaim in Australia and around the world. She was awarded the Commonwealth Writers' Prize for *Too Many Men*, and France's Prix Médicis Étranger for *Lola Bensky*. Lily Brett is married to the Australian painter David Rankin. They have three children and live in New York.

lilybrett.com

LILY BRETT

Old Seems
to be
Other People

HAMISH HAMILTON
an imprint of
PENGUIN BOOKS

HAMISH HAMILTON

UK | USA | Canada| Ireland | Australia
India | New Zealand | South Africa | China

Hamish Hamilton is part of the Penguin Random House group of companies
whose addresses can be found at global.penguinrandomhouse.com.

Penguin
Random House
Australia

First published by Hamish Hamilton, 2021

Cover design by Alex Ross © Penguin Random House Australia Pty Ltd
Cover portrait *Aqua Lily* by David Rankin; *High-angle View of Manhattan's
Skyscrapers* courtesy Getty Images
Typeset in Adobe Caslon Pro by Midland Typesetters, Australia
Printed and bound in Australia by Griffin Press, part of Ovato, an accredited
ISO AS/NZS 14001 Environmental Management Systems printer

A catalogue record for this
book is available from the
National Library of Australia

ISBN 978 1 76104 234 8

penguin.com.au

MIX
Paper from
responsible sources
FSC® C009448

For David, whom I fell in love with two, or maybe it was three, days after we met.

And for my darling friend, Audette Exel, who founded the Adara Group.

Contents

Harder

It is easier to feel young in New York. There is, in this city, almost an insistence, if not a belief, that everyone is young. 'Young lady' is a common form of address. 'How can I help you, young lady?' the man at my local drycleaner's asks me when I walk into his store. Often it is early in the morning and I want to laugh. I am not young. I am in my late sixties.

It is not that I feel old. I should feel old, but I don't. Parts of me still feel the same as I did in my twenties. I am, despite having spent half of my adult life and three quarters of my income on psychoanalysis, still indecisive, hesitant, bothered or anxious too much of the time.

It is harder to feel old in New York. Another frequently used term of address in New York is 'Miss'. Good morning, Miss. Excuse me, Miss. 'Miss' applies to you whether you are ten and have braces on your teeth or eighty and need a cane.

The terminology used here is perennially youthful. Women of any age can refer to their 'boyfriend'. The word 'boyfriend' could be seen as belonging to adolescence. But not in New York. You can be dating someone even if you are in your seventies, eighties or nineties.

My husband and I were at the Cupping Room Cafe, a very old, unpretentious restaurant in SoHo. I was feeling a bit flat. My doctor had said I had to have an ultrasound sonogram of my renal arteries. He thought one of them might be narrowing. I hadn't even known I had renal arteries. I try not to think too much about my body – how many of our body parts have to be working in perfect harmony and symmetry in order for us to do anything. I had been fretting about this possible narrowing of my newly discovered renal arteries.

We had just sat down when I looked up and felt that something was wrong. The other diners didn't look like the regular clientele. They weren't. The waiter told me they were participants in a speed-dating dinner. A speed-dating dinner. I was intrigued. I left my husband and moved closer to the action. Each of the speed-dating dinner guests spent six minutes with one of the other guests of the opposite sex. After six minutes they had to change partners.

I was mesmerised. All of the women had dressed up. You could see that they had made an effort. The men hadn't bothered. They knew that they didn't have to. They knew that as long as they were still breathing they were desirable. I watched the women trying so hard and the men looking laidback. I was watching so intently that the man running the speed-dating dinner came over and asked me if I was interested in joining a speed-dating dinner. They had, he said, speed-dating events for all ages. And a relatively high rate of successful matches, he added.

It is really hard to feel old or worry about a renal artery when you've just been invited to a speed-dating dinner.

Dickens Street

It is not always easy to face your past. Our past, for most of us, has uncomfortable and unpalatable moments. For years, I simultaneously felt homesick and dreaded the thought of returning to Melbourne. As though it was only the geographical distance that separated me from my past and not the years or decades that had passed.

I have lived in New York for over thirty years, yet I still feel as though New York contains my present. My past is in Melbourne. The truth is that it is hard to avoid your past. For most of us, it is always present.

When I was fourteen, we moved from a small cottage in the inner-suburban, then very working-class suburb of North Carlton, to Elwood, a more middle-class suburb on the other side of the city.

The new house seemed enormous to me. It had three bedrooms, a living and dining room, a large kitchen and an indoor toilet. At night, I no longer had to unlock the back door and go outside to the toilet, which had been next to a pile of coal that seemed to be a playground for the local rats.

We lived in Dickens Street. Dickens Street was surrounded by, among others, Wordsworth, Tennyson, Milton, Scott, Shelley, Keats, Browning, Bronte, Burns and Shakespeare streets. The streets were named by the local council in the 1850s in order to uplift the character of the residents of Elwood, who were deemed to be a bunch of cantankerous malcontents. It must have worked as all our neighbours seemed very nice and I don't think I saw even one cantankerous malcontent.

A few years ago, for the first time in almost twenty years, I went back to that house. I was so nervous about going inside. As though my past was lodged in the house and not in my heart.

In front of the front door was a wrought-iron gate with a wrought-iron peacock in the centre of the gate. The doorbell still had the same chimes. I felt both very moved and very anxious at the sound of those chimes. I hadn't yet entered the house.

The kitchen was what I dreaded most. The kitchen had been my mother's domain. It was where she peeled and chopped vegetables and fruit. It was where she ground veal and beef and added onions, eggs and breadcrumbs to make meatballs and meatloaves. And where she baked sponge cakes so light that my father and I were banished from the kitchen in case our footsteps deflated the cake.

Stepping into the house, I felt overwhelmed by something I had never noticed. The house was just beautiful. I must have been blinded by my teenage years or my repressed anxiety and anger. I was stunned at the carefully crafted and designed details everywhere I looked.

The deep-blue carpet in the hallway and living and dining room was so plush that almost six decades later, it still looked new. Indented in the carpet were a series of rectangular shapes that were beside and inside each other.

The glass walls of the shower were sandblasted and the floor was tiled with small pink, grey and black tiles, each individually placed in a pattern that looked as though the tiles had been woven together.

Every light fitting was beautiful. Even the handles of the drawers and cupboards seemed to be in tune with the rest of the house, which had been carefully maintained by the new owner.

Finally, I walked into the kitchen. I could hardly breathe. I looked around and was shocked at the realisation that the stove had six burners. At the time I had lived there, no one in Melbourne, except for restaurants or the very wealthy, had a six-burner stove.

I half expected my mother to appear, and wished that she could. I wanted to cry for having blocked out the extraordinary feat my father had achieved in building the house. My father was not a man who was interested in anything to do with architecture or design. I knew he had hired an architect. And I knew that he had, after work, regularly driven straight to the construction site that was going to be our new home.

He climbed up ladders and examined the shells of the walls and the ceilings and the beams. My father knew nothing about construction. But he wanted to know everything about the construction of this house. What I knew at the time, and what was blazingly clear now, was that the house was built out of my father's deep and undying love for my mother.

I moved out of that house when I was nineteen. At twenty-one, I married an Australian rock musician. I decided to get pregnant and then we left for London. Not long after that, I gave birth to a baby boy. The marriage didn't last which, in hindsight, was not surprising.

I moved back to Melbourne when my small, beautiful boy was eighteen months old. This boy changed my mother's life. My mother fell in love with him the moment she saw him. He gave her a happiness that seemed to fill a part of the void left by the loss of her parents, her siblings, her aunts, uncles, cousins, nephews, nieces and the loss of her youth and her education.

I had no idea why I had decided to get pregnant when I was so young and so newly married. When I saw my mother with my son, I understood that I had had him for her. I loved him with all my heart, and I knew that he was partly hers. My son was a medical student when my mother died. He sat beside her and stroked her hand as she lay dying, at sixty-four. I wept for years after her death.

My mother spent the last few months of her life telling every doctor or passer-by that her son was a medical student. She often called him her son. I never minded.

Twenty-two years after her death, my mother's eyes arrived on a small girl, the first-born child of my child, the son who had filled part of that void in my mother's heart. This small girl was born with a sureness and a radiance, and she has stayed that way.

She is now twelve and her smile, which could light up the universe, reminds me of my mother in the only photograph I have of her before her world cracked and crashed. In the photograph, my mother is fourteen and on a school outing from Lodz to Warsaw. My mother who was born in Lodz, Poland, had never been out of Lodz. My mother looks so exited and full of life. Her smile is contagious. Her arm is around the schoolfriend who gave me the photo.

Cher

I am sitting in a nondescript deli/cafe on Fourteenth Street. A man in his early thirties, at the next table, is having an earnest conversation about Cher. I am pleased that Cher is still being talked about with such earnestness. I interviewed Cher, several times, in the late 1960s, when I was a rock journalist. I feel a degree of pleasure in her accomplishments.

'Cher is ninety-three,' the man says to the young woman, who has been glued to his every word. She looks impressed. 'Cher is ninety-three and she still has a thick head of hair,' he says. I glare at him. He doesn't notice. Cher and I are exactly the same age. Neither of us is ninety-three. I feel affronted on Cher's behalf. It is bothering enough being older without being mistaken for a 93-year-old.

A friend has recently advised me to never look in a mirror while wearing my glasses. I didn't bother to explain to her that without my glasses I wouldn't be able to see that much. I think she meant well. I already frown when I look at myself in the mirror, although I have probably been doing that for most of my life.

Being older bothers me more than I let myself know. In the supermarket, I stride past the ever-increasing shelves of incontinence pads as though if I paused or even walked too close my bladder might take it upon itself to begin to leak.

I leave the cafe. I have an appointment with my dermatologist for a regular check-up. I try to erase all thoughts of Cher or myself being ninety-three.

I am at the dermatologist. I am standing, almost naked, while he looks carefully all over my body. He is wearing magnifying goggles, the sort that look as though they could see right through several layers of epidermis to your liver or your lungs.

He finishes his examination, steps back and says, 'You look in great shape.'

I look at him. 'No-one in their right mind would look at me, naked, and say that,' I say. And it is true. Everything on my body is lower and a lot less firm than it used to be.

He laughs. I realise he was speaking in dermatological terms. He meant that he couldn't see anything worrying on my skin.

This being New York, my dermatologist lives in the same building as Keith Richards. He tells me that he has given Keith – he calls him Keith, as though Keith was Keith Brown or Keith Smith – a copy of my novel, *Lola Bensky*. *Lola Bensky* is loosely, or not so loosely, based on my life as a very young rock journalist.

My husband is a painter. He loves the Rolling Stones. He listens to the Rolling Stones while he is painting, in his studio. He has the volume turned up as high as it can go. I try hard to avoid hearing even one note. Except when Keith Richards sings about the need to move, to live, to have fun, while you still can.

That note stays in my head.

Small Moments

My happiest memories are made up of small moments. Maybe the fact that I am no longer forty or fifty or even sixty makes me more appreciative of these moments. For a big city, New York is surprisingly full of small moments.

In this bustling, relatively restless metropolis, small moments seem even more amplified. A few years ago, in the middle of an early-morning rush hour, I bumped into my daughter on Sixth Avenue. We were both so startled and so happy to have this unexpected meeting. We hugged each other while others swarmed past us. She was on her way to work and I blew her kisses until she disappeared into the Ninth Street PATH station entrance.

In a city of over eight-and-a-half million people, the chances of bumping into your daughter are slim. New York is the most densely populated city in the US.

About one in every thirty-eight people in the US lives in New York. There are twenty-seven thousand people per square mile.

Even so, you can't count on anonymity in this city. I have bumped into my literary agent in a small bra store on University Place. Trying on bras always leaves me red-faced and flustered. A bra store is not an ideal place to have a chat with your literary agent. Especially if that chat is about why your new novel isn't yet finished.

And, in a particularly packed part of Fourteenth Street, I managed to walk straight into someone I was trying hard to avoid.

There are also small, almost subliminal moments in the city that connect us to each other. A wordless tolerance and acceptance of the fact that we are all standing and waiting on an almost airless subway platform on a very hot, humid day, or freezing on that platform in winter.

And we share an understanding of the small and large idiosyncrasies of the city. You can see, as I did recently, a beautiful, young ballerina in a fluffy pink tutu and pink satin ballet shoes crossing Houston Street at a relatively gritty intersection. The ballerina was carrying an equally fluffy white dog adorned with pink ribbons. Nobody except me thought this was strange.

I was also the only one glued to the sight of a dog being photographed in a park on the Lower East Side.

This dog was a professional. When the photographer said, 'Look left', the dog looked left. On command, the dog could look left or right or look straight ahead. He could also lift his chin a little higher or look pensively down at the ground. Looking pensive can't be easy to interpret if you are a dog.

Some small moments are larger than others. The day my husband called to say he wanted to marry me, I had sixteen frozen pheasants floating in the bath. The pheasants were supposed to have been delivered fresh, not frozen. Having sixteen frozen pheasants floating in your bath can be very unsettling. And, I had thirty-two people coming to dinner.

'I love you,' he said. 'I want to marry you.'

I stopped talking about the pheasants. The pheasants were not my biggest problem. I had a more pressing problem. I was married to someone else.

I have never cooked pheasant again.

Friends

I am on the F Train, the subway line that services the Lower East Side, where I now live. It is early-morning rush hour. The train is crowded. Jam-packed. No-one offers me their seat. This is not a matter of rudeness. New Yorkers, on the whole, are not rude. They assume that if you are a New Yorker you are just as capable of doing anything as any other New Yorker. And that includes standing up on the subway. I quite like that assumption, except when I am dying to sit down.

My husband and I have to be on the Upper East Side in twenty-five minutes. We need to switch to the 6 Train. My husband thinks he knows which subway stop will connect us to the 6 Train. I am not sure. I want to ask someone. My husband doesn't. He hates asking for directions. I don't know why. Why are so many men averse to asking for directions?

I ask a woman standing next to me about the 6 Train. It turns out that my husband is right about the connection. The woman has a slight Russian accent. She is in her fifties and wearing an interesting coat.

'Are you Russian?' I say to her.

'Russian Jewish,' she says.

'Polish Jewish,' I answer.

I am surprised at myself. I hardly ever talk to strangers. Two minutes later we have established that we are practically neighbours. She tells me her name is Galina.

This startles me at first. I used the name Galina to disguise my Russian pedicurist, whom I had quoted in my book, *Only In New York*, as saying that she doesn't like sex. Not many women, especially married women, will tell you that they don't like sex. But my Russian pedicurist was adamant about the fact that she didn't like sex.

I feel guilty, as though I had quoted this Galina talking about not liking sex and not my disguised Russian pedicurist.

Just before I get off the train, I write my name and email address on a scrap of paper, and write her email address on another scrap. It feels like an audacious move. The sort of move you make more easily when you are a teenager or in your twenties or thirties.

Somehow, by the time you are sixty, and certainly by the time you are almost seventy, it becomes much harder to make new friends. I mean close friends. The sort of friends with whom you talk about *everything*.

I have some very dear close friends. Friends I love. But most of them live in other countries. I miss them. I sound a bit plaintive when I talk about how much I miss them.

I think about Galina on and off during the day. In the late afternoon I send her an email. She writes back. We arrange to meet for dinner the following week.

She tells me that she and her husband go bike riding along the East River. She rides a three-wheeler. A tricycle? I have been thinking about buying a tricycle for years and years. A fear of looking really stupid has stopped me. Galina emails me a photo of her tricycle. She says we could ride along the East River together.

I go online and find the tricycle. It is on sale. I order one.

The Apple Store

I walked into the Apple store, in SoHo. The Apple store was very crowded. It was seven p.m. There were lines of people waiting for an Apple assistant to assist them with their laptop, tablet or smartphone problem.

I looked around and realised, with a jolt, that I was the oldest person in the store. I am not ninety-nine. Until a few weeks ago, I was still in my sixties. Two Apple assistants approached me. They were both young men. I could tell that they took one look at me and decided it would take two of them to help me with my technology issues.

I needed help setting up my new iPad. I had to make sure that all the correspondence and information on my old iPad was transferred. The Apple assistants sat me down at a long bench and gave me several simple instructions on how to begin.

'Good job,' they said, after I had completed the first simple step of the set-up of my new iPad. Good job. They said this in the tone of voice you would use if you were speaking to a three-year-old.

'Really good job,' they said, in unison, several steps later.

A few other customers waiting in line were, I thought, glaring at me and possibly wondering why I needed two Apple assistants. I had almost completed the set-up when one of the Apple assistants apologised to me for having to leave. His apology was very pained. As though he was a cardiothoracic surgeon having to leave in the middle of a complex pulmonary or cardiac procedure. It was, he explained, his fiancée's birthday. 'You are doing so well,' he said as he left.

Finally, my new iPad was set up. 'Great job,' the other assistant said. 'It was a pleasure to help you,' he added. By now, I was feeling like a relic from the Palaeolithic era. I strode home at twice the pace I normally walk as though to prove to myself that I wasn't yet geriatric.

I don't usually feel old. I have trouble feeling old. I am sometimes shocked that I have just turned seventy and feel not quite sure how I reached this age with such lightning speed. On the whole, I feel a sort of indeterminate age.

A day later, I was in Midtown, on Lexington Avenue. I was waiting for the Hampton Jitney, a bus that runs between Manhattan and the South and North Forks of Long Island. The Hamptons, on the South Fork, have a lot of celebrities and people who own yachts. The North Fork is more rural and, to me, more desirable.

The North Fork Jitney is late. I call the bus company. 'Where is the bus?' I say. 'It is raining and there are several elderly people in the line'. She tells me the bus will be there in ten minutes. It suddenly dawns on me that I am the same age as the people I described as elderly.

According to the World Health Organization, most developed countries accept the age of sixty-five and over as the definition of elderly. Last month, my six-year-old grandson, who was visiting from San Francisco, leaped into my bed at five a.m. in the morning.

'Why are your arms floppy?' he asked.

'Because I am elderly,' I said.

Happy

By February, we have all said 'Happy New Year' to each other dozens of times. As the last of the Happy New Years faded, I read an article saying that research by the US Centers for Disease Control and Prevention suggested that New York was number one on the list of the top-ten unhappiest cities in the US.

This shocked me. I knew it couldn't possibly be true. I asked a very smart young friend. He agreed it couldn't possibly be true. He rattled off an impressive series of statistics, including the city's low unemployment and crime rate. If New Yorkers were so unhappy, he added, why was the city's population growing so rapidly?

I looked more closely at the research. I immediately saw the flaw. The data the researchers used was self-reported. No self-respecting New Yorker would admit to being happy. We love to complain. We love to complain about our city, our job, our state of mind and our health. We complain whether we are twenty-five or eighty-five.

I complain a lot. I also don't mind other people complaining. In a strange way, you get to know people more intimately, I think, if you listen to their complaints. My husband, as I have noted before, says that if I had been born in the Brontë sisters' time I would have written *Bothering Heights*, not *Wuthering Heights*. *Bothering Heights* would clearly have been full of complaints.

My father never complains. He celebrated his one-hundreth birthday last July. He is always happy to see me. Always cheerful. He is a great role model for how to age with grace. I know that if I ever live to that sort of old age, I will not be like him. I have warned my children that I will be very grumpy and full of complaints.

My father had such a great time at his one-hundreth birthday party. He loved the magician we had hired to perform at the party and my father clapped as hard as any of the six of his eight grandchildren who were at the party. He also ate at least a quarter of the very rich Imperial Torte that a friend had air-freighted to him from Vienna. I decided that there was no point in telling a 100-year-old man that he is eating too much cake.

My father is a man who had every reason to not be able to feel joy. He spent just over five years imprisoned in a Nazi ghetto, labour camp and death camp. Most of his family were murdered. But for most of my life my father has had a great appetite, a love of beautiful women and a great sense of humour.

My father moved to New York when he was in his late eighties. He loved the fact that when I took him clothes shopping, perfect strangers would smile at me and say, 'Bless you'.

New Yorkers, it seems to me, are made happy by the small, almost invisible activities – like a daughter taking her elderly father out shopping for clothes or shoes – that we see almost every day. New Yorkers are definitely no less happy than anyone else. They may not easily admit their happiness, but if you live here, it is palpable.

City Life

Most people think of country life as being healthier, cleaner, more invigorating. Not me. Put me too close to a tree, and while others are admiring the view I am feeling ill at ease and sneezing. Also, all hills, meadows and valleys look the same to me. I can't tell the difference between a paddock and a prairie. And I find it difficult to distinguish one tree from another.

I like proximity to hospitals and twenty-four-hour urgent-care clinics. I don't particularly want to go to a hospital or urgent-care clinic, I just like to know they are close by. In New York, we have plenty of both, although I did briefly contemplate moving to Seattle when I read, a few years ago, that Seattle had one of the fastest ambulance response rates in the US.

I love cities. Particularly densely populated cities like New York.

In New York, it is harder to dwell on how old you are, something I have been doing more frequently since I turned seventy last year. There is an agelessness in being part of a diverse, small or large crowd of people. You become immersed in the experience you are collectively sharing and not your own or anyone else's particular age.

I was watching a large, brown rat walking slowly back and forth along the subway tracks at the Second Avenue subway station. About a dozen other people on the platform were also watching the rat. We looked at the rat, looked at each other and looked back at the rat. One young woman stepped further back on the platform. I didn't.

I am no longer afraid of rats. I lost my fear when I read that New York's brown rats are not particularly bold. They take at least two days to touch a new object or to even try unfamiliar food. I also read that they have a life span of only one year, and rarely walk more than six hundred feet from where they were born. That sort of information can really change your attitude to rats.

There is also, in New York, always something to divert you. Last week, I came across a bargain store in the basement of what was a former synagogue and is now a Buddhist temple. I was thrilled enough about this interconnection of religious beliefs but then I walked into the basement store.

The store was packed with very cheap, brightly coloured plastic buckets and bowls and kitchen utensils. I love brightly coloured plastic kitchen utensils. Not many of my friends share this love. My kitchen has more than a dozen plastic egg separators, mixing spoons and potato mashers. I bought them all in a small Mexican mountain town. I am not sure why I bought so many potato mashers. I never mash potatoes.

The basement store underneath the Buddhist temple also sold groceries, detergents, stationery, candy, clothes, coats, shoes and several wedding dresses. I could have spent hours there but I had already bought too many plastic salad servers, spatulas and measuring spoons.

I walked home with a spring in my step and the sound of Buddhist chants interspersed with taxi horns.

Walking

I love walking. Particularly in cities. I discovered the joy of walking relatively late in life. I was in my early forties. I grew up with a father who never walked if he could drive. He would do two U-turns and drive half a block to pick up some milk and I would do more or less the same until I moved to New York.

You are almost forced to walk if you live in New York. There is no way to avoid it. You can't just get in a car and drive everywhere. You would never get there – and if you did, there would be nowhere to park the car.

Whatever your age, and particularly if you are older, walking is good for you. New York is a perfect city for walking. The streets of the city are a constantly changing piece of theatre. Every few steps there is another view, another setting, another tableau. There are no relentless stretches of indistinguishable streets.

There is a lot of movement. There are cars, people, buses, bikes. The people are walking at varying speeds, each with their own stride and gait. And there is your own movement, which becomes part of the whole momentum.

There is also a background of sound. An almost melodic composition of cars, trucks, buses, taxi horns, the low rumbling of the subway, people humming or singing to whatever music they are listening to and the occasional siren of an ambulance or fire truck.

This choreography of sound and movement could seem chaotic and distressing, but it isn't. It has a symphonic synergy, a finely synchronised order almost as smooth as the miraculous workings of a cardiovascular or gastrointestinal system.

The visual aspect of the city adds to the action. There are signs and posters and messages and directions everywhere. On taxis, buses, storefronts, walls, doors and scaffolding.

My dentist would periodically pause, often in the middle of one of the complex dental procedures I was undergoing, and say, 'I really should have gone into the scaffolding business.' He would be looking wistfully out of the window at the scaffolding around a New York University building. The scaffolding had been there for years while the planned construction work still hadn't even started.

I tried not to think about the fact that my dentist was looking out of the window instead of into my mouth.

Or that he would have preferred a scaffolding business instead of dentistry.

Another aspect of the symmetry of New York is that most of the streets of the city are on a horizontal and vertical grid. This makes it easier for people like me to not get lost. I can get lost anywhere. I can get lost in an aeroplane. If I leave my seat to go to the bathroom, I can have trouble relocating where I was sitting.

I also can't grasp geography. My husband has drawn endless maps of Europe for me, yet I still ask him if Italy shares a border with Croatia or whether Hamburg is close to Hungary.

My last psychoanalyst – and I have had three – suggested that my problem with geography was linked to the fact that my mother and father were each imprisoned in Nazi ghettos and death camps, and therefore the map of Europe looked chaotic and bewildering to me.

For years I toyed with the idea of blaming Hitler for my geographic confusion. However, whichever way I look at it, I can't really blame him for the fact that I can easily get lost in a hotel and can't find my way back to my seat in an aeroplane.

Discrepancies

I don't like mirrors. I try to avoid them. My husband has noted, more than once, that I must have no idea of what I look like because I frown and grimace at myself every time I look in a mirror. I tried to practise smiling when I approached a mirror, but I just looked deranged – and possibly dangerous.

Even so, I spend a lot longer looking in the mirror and making small adjustments to my appearance before leaving the house than my husband ever does.

Why is it that, regardless of our age, in order to be seen as attractive or to be considered marriageable, women have to do their hair, watch their weight, wear flattering clothes, perfume, moisturise and deodorise ourselves while men can be unkempt, untidy, ungroomed and, even worse, unwashed, they can still be seen as – as a friend of mine put it – 'a good catch'.

In the US, and I suspect this is probably true of most Western countries, older men are much more likely to be married than older women. Recent statistics show that about seventy-five per cent of men aged from sixty-five to seventy-four are married, compared to fifty-eight per cent of women.

The percentage of men aged seventy-four to eighty-five who are married doesn't drop at all, while the percentage of married women of that age plummets to forty-two per cent. And the numbers get worse. Sixty per cent of men over the age of eighty-five are married but only seventeen per cent of women that age are married.

Why is it that men, unlike women, don't seem to have a use-by date? Men's use-by date seems to end only with their own expiration.

Men are obviously still marrying younger women. They always have – I cheer every time I hear of an older man marrying someone more or less his own age. Women also tend to marry men older than themselves. And women live longer. But all of that can't account for the large discrepancies in marital status.

New York has a reputation as a city in which it is difficult for single women to meet available men. There are nearly 400 000 more women than men in New York. In a population that is bigger than the population of Austria, Ireland or many other countries, that number should be insignificant.

Half of all New Yorkers speak a language other than English at home. There are over two hundred languages spoken in this city. You would think with all of this diversity that it would be as easy for older women to find a partner as it is for older men. But it isn't.

Of course not all women want a partner. One of my older friends is eighty and widowed. The first time I saw her after her husband had died was at lunch at a restaurant in the East Village. I had been worried about her. Worried that she would be fragile and subdued.

She was hugging me before I recognised her. She had a new haircut, new clothes and a jauntiness about her that I had never seen before. 'I'm having the time of my life,' she said. She invited me to dinner the following week. 'I'm inviting people who Norbert hated,' she added. Norbert was her relatively recently departed husband. I laughed because the idea of that sort of dinner party was funny and not because Norbert clearly hadn't liked me.

The Shower

I have a new shower. A new shower is not something New Yorkers get very excited about. Mention a balcony, a view, a garden or a bedroom bigger than a matchbox and you will have a receptive audience. New Yorkers are galvanised by talk about real estate.

I love my new shower. I am unashamedly attached to this new shower. I don't usually form attachments to material possessions. My attachments are mostly to people. I don't mind if anyone breaks one of my glasses or dishes or vases, or scratches a surface.

I am also happy to share almost everything I have. Except for my new shower. I have, so far, managed to avoid letting anyone else use it. Luckily, we have two bathrooms.

I didn't choose this shower. The contractor who renovated the apartment did. He is a tall, big, burly man. He asked what sort of shower I wanted. I said one you could walk into. If you are over sixty, it is probably best, if you can avoid it, to not have to step over a bath to get into the shower.

This contractor is very smart. He can calculate, in his head, how much timber it takes to build a deck, a house or kilometres of bookshelves, in two minutes. You don't have to tell him anything twice. My request was for a shower. And I got one. I was going away for a week. He said the new shower would be installed when I got back. And it was.

This shower is not an ordinary shower. It can do things other showers can't. It has a shower massage panel with a digital thermometer, six adjustable spray massage jets, an adjustable, multi-functional showerhead, a hand shower with a chrome-plated brass hose almost two metres long, and a fog-free mirror. You can see why I am thrilled – although I could do without the fog-free mirror. I am not prone to looking at myself, unclothed, in a mirror. And anyway, when you are well over sixty, it is not a good idea to look at yourself when you are naked. Especially if you are wearing reading glasses. The shower also has a three-way diverted valve to control water operations. I have no idea what that means but it sounds impressive and is possibly essential.

The shower also looks really impressive. When anyone sees it, I feel a need to explain that I didn't choose it.

And that the contractor got it at a special sale price, which is true. I don't want to be seen as a person who needs a flashy shower. I also don't mention how much I love the shower for fear of looking even more superficial.

But I do love this shower. The contractor set the shower at a perfect temperature. Now, I happily shower with water that is never too hot or too cold. And I feel full of admiration for what this shower can do. I, however, do nothing other than turn on the water and enjoy the shower. I am way too nervous to adjust the multi-functional showerhead or use the hand shower or touch any of the other profusion of settings.

Franz Joseph Haydn

I was asked to write an essay for a book about Haydn. Franz Joseph Haydn, the composer. I was flattered but I said that I was not the right person to write an essay about Haydn – in fact, I was the last person in the world who should be asked to write an essay about Haydn.

Eight emails later, despite the fact that I had explained that I never listen to music, they insisted that I was the perfect person to write the essay. I gave up. I am not sure that they fully grasped the fact that I don't listen to music.

I listen to words in the way other people listen to music. Maybe getting lost in music is something I am afraid of, while getting lost in the sound of words is, for me, something quite sublime.

I put words together and pull them apart in my head. I love the rhythm of words. I can listen to people speaking languages I don't understand and enjoy the sounds and the melody.

I envy people who can lose themselves in music. Music is an extraordinarily swift way of being transported to something more elevated than most of our everyday activities.

I can't easily get lost. I have to be on guard. On guard for what isn't exactly clear. But it does stem from having two parents who were imprisoned for years in Nazi ghettos and death camps.

I can, however, get lost in writing. I don't know what it is about words that gives me a feeling of safety and what it is about music that frightens me. I think it is the instant power of music. Music can catch you unawares. It can seep into you in a second and grab you abruptly and unprepared.

A New York City taxicab driver once asked me if I liked opera. He didn't wait for my answer before telling me he was listening to Maria Callas singing the Puccini aria, 'Un Bel Di, Vedremo', from *Madame Butterfly*.

I started weeping two minutes after Maria Callas started singing. By the time I reached my destination my eyes were swollen and I had run out of tissues.

'It is not as wild or dramatic when sung by some others,' the driver said as I was paying the fare.

Wild and dramatic? I thought Callas's voice was filled with tragedy and a raw desperation.

'She died in 1977 of a heart attack at fifty-three,' the driver called out to me. That made me feel even worse.

Having agreed to write an essay about Haydn, I needed to understand at least a little about Haydn's music. I called my friend Howie. Howie is a rabbi, a lawyer, a linguist, a musician and a recently retired member of a drag a cappella group. I had done a little research. I asked Howie what the difference would be between 'Solo e Pensoso', a poem written by Francesco Petrarch in about 1337, as set to music by Luca Marenzio and then turned into an aria by Haydn. I felt very smart just for being able to ask that question.

'You should probably download both pieces and listen to them, in succession,' Howie said. 'I just listened to snippets of both of them and the body sensation you get from each of them is quite different,' he added.

I was already in trouble. I had no idea what Howie was talking about. 'Could you tell me exactly what that *body sensation* feels like?' I said.

Howie sighed. 'You have to feel it,' he said.

That was not a helpful reply. How would I feel my body sensation if I don't know what to look for? I tried again. 'What did you feel?' I asked Howie.

'The Marenzio piece hit me on the skin and caused a pressure behind the tear ducts, the Haydn piece warmed me.'

A pressure behind the tear ducts? I didn't even know where my tear ducts were. I knew they were in the vicinity of my eyes and not around my waist or my ankles. I looked up 'tear ducts' in my medical encyclopedia. Yes, I own the *American College of Physicians Complete Home Medical Guide*.

It seemed as though the tear ducts were about three quarters of the way down the side of the nose. That hadn't helped. I was pretty sure that I had never felt a pressure behind that part of my nose.

My research into Haydn was going nowhere. I read some of Haydn's letters. I discovered that Haydn loved writing. He often wrote about the events of his life in notebooks. I felt an immediate affinity with him. I love notebooks.

I also read that Beethoven, at nineteen, travelled to Vienna to learn from Haydn. Beethoven wanted to learn more about the technical aspects of music and Haydn, who was already technically brilliant, was more interested in the emotional impact music had on the audience. I liked Haydn more and more.

I learned that at eight Haydn was living with his father's cousin and singing in the choir of St Stephen's Cathedral, in Vienna. He sang in the cathedral choir for nine years and studied religion, mathematics, Latin, writing, violin, clavier and voice. He taught himself music theory and composition. That is pretty impressive. When I was eight,

I was practising forging my mother's and father's signatures. How I used that skill is a long story.

Haydn married his wife, Maria Anna Keller, in St Stephen's Cathedral. No-one seemed to definitively know why Haydn married Maria Anna Keller but there seemed to be a consensus that the marriage was not a happy one. Maria Anna is invariably described as awful and having no respect for Haydn's talent. She was said to do things like use his compositions to line her cake tins or tear the compositions into strips to curl her hair.

I felt sorry for Haydn, who stayed married to Maria Anna Keller until her death. That is, until I learned that Haydn had several mistresses over the years. *Several* mistresses? If I was Maria Anna, I would be using his compositions to curl my hair more frequently and baking as many cakes as I could.

Haydn wrote beautiful love letters. Not to Maria Anna. I read some of the letters he wrote to Maria Anna von Genziger, a Viennese married mother of six children. In his first letter to Maria Anna von Genziger, he commented on her handwriting. 'Nothing delighted me more,' he said, 'than the surprise of seeing such lovely handwriting.' I love men who love handwriting, but I was not overlooking Haydn's mistresses.

In another letter to von Genziger, Haydn wrote of feeling melancholy. He said he felt forsaken like some sort of poor orphan. Possibly everyone other than the most overt extrovert has experienced this sort of loneliness. The pain of loneliness is, I think, as piercing as any physical ailment or injury.

Haydn told von Genziger that her comforting letters cheered him up. He said they were highly necessary for his heart, which was often deeply hurt. Although I was not ignoring his infidelity, I was touched that he could write so intimately about his feelings. We don't talk or write to each other like that anymore.

Haydn spent a year or two in London. While he was there he met Rebecca Schroeter. Rebecca Schroeter's letters to Haydn are heartfelt declarations of love. She told him that no language could express half the love and affection she felt for him. She told him in her letters that he was dearer to her every day of her life.

Haydn copied these letters into his notebooks. That is an act as romantic as any act of love I know. The thought of Haydn transposing Rebecca Schroeter's letters into his notebook was very moving.

By the time I had read Haydn's letters to Maria Anna von Genziger and Rebecca Schroeter's letters, I was in love with Haydn. His adultery had faded into the background. I loved his directness, his passion and his courage in expressing his feelings.

Now that I had formed this attachment to Haydn, I knew that I really should listen to some of his music.

I decided to listen to Leonard Bernstein conducting the Bayerischer Rundfunk's orchestra and choir in *Die Schöpfung*. I don't know why. It was probably because I loved the sounds of the Rundfunk and *Die Schöpfung*. I put on headphones so I could hear *Die Schöpfung* very clearly. The music started and I frowned. I ignored my frown. I found the music strangely soothing.

I thought I would listen for ten or twenty minutes. I looked at my watch and saw that I had listened to *Die Schöpfung* for almost ninety minutes. I took a break. The experience had been not too bad. I felt proud of myself and planned to do this again.

The people who commissioned the essay were pleased with the essay. They said mine was a very different way of looking at Haydn. I was thrilled.

The plan to listen to music didn't quite work out. Instead I began reading the letters of Beethoven, Mozart and Chopin. I now know much more about music.

Love

I have lived in New York for almost thirty years. I love this city. But, like all love affairs, whether they are fleeting or last a lifetime, there are moments of tension. Moments when you blame the other person for everything. Or worse, moments when you can't remember why you love them.

It is the same with New York. Some days the city drives me crazy. Some days I think I am crazy to live here. The noise feels louder, the traffic appears to be more congested. The streets seem more crowded. The crowded streets are not just an illusion. Last year New York had sixty million visitors. That is like having the entire population of Italy visit you in one year.

For the singer Paul Simon, the city's streets are never too loud or too crowded. He sings about hearing a gospel hymn in the city's crowds and not being alone because New York is his home.

Not being alone is part of the reason that more and more people over sixty are staying in the city. In previous decades retirement meant leaving for Florida or moving to the suburbs. It is harder to be alone in New York. Apart from the easy access to the city's cultural events, quite a few of which are free, there are so many people. Step outside your front door and sooner or later someone will talk to you.

The film director Sydney Lumet was succinct about his attachment to this metropolis: 'I'm not comfortable any place but New York,' he said. 'When I leave New York for any other place in the United States, my nose starts to bleed.'

Most New Yorkers have come from somewhere else. I moved here from Australia. It was not my idea to move to New York. It was my husband who dreamt of living here.

For the first year or two, I was miserable. I missed my friends. I even missed people I didn't like. Being surrounded by some people you dislike seems part of a well-rounded life, to me. And then, almost without noticing it, I fell in love with the city.

Newcomers to this city soon become New Yorkers. We absorb many of the characteristics of being a New Yorker. We talk a lot. We argue a lot – but it is okay to voice dissenting opinions here. We also don't panic easily.

Just over a year ago, a homemade pressure-cooker bomb exploded on West 23rd Street. Luckily no-one was seriously injured. 'Chelsea Bombing' was the headline in all the news outlets. I brought up the bombing with an 82-year-old friend of mine. Her response was to inform me that that part of West 23rd Street was not in Chelsea.

The Twitter responses to the Chelsea Bombing were similar. 'Please don't spread misinformation about the bomb. It is the Flatiron District, not Chelsea' and 'Dear Media, 23rd Street and 6th Avenue is Flatiron not Chelsea' were not uncommon responses. The tweets made me laugh. I was not laughing about the bomb. I was laughing at the lack of panic. And the fact that we can maintain our sense of humour and take a stand against hateful intentions.

I am prone to panic. About everything. Some of the city's lack of panic has rubbed off on me. I am calmer than I used to be. Living in New York has clearly been good for me.

Advice

My first job was as a rock journalist. I was not a journalist. I didn't know I could write. And I had never used a typewriter or a tape recorder. A real journalist, an older man who worked at another newspaper, gave me a tip: 'Always begin with a good first line,' he said. I took that tip seriously. I felt more equipped to begin my life as a rock journalist.

Around the same time, a friend and I were talking about marriage. We were nineteen. Neither of us was married. I was talking about love, when she looked at me and said, 'If you can't stand the way he eats, then the marriage is in trouble.' This thought lodged itself in my head.

I have been married to my husband for a long time. We have seen each other eat approximately 103 800 times. I have never had a problem with the way he eats. Although I do, periodically, mid-meal, check to make sure nothing has changed.

We all dispense advice. Especially New Yorkers. New Yorkers will tell you what subway lines to avoid, where to get the best bagels or pizza, what movies to see and offer endless advice about politics and the weather.

My doctor told me that that the Doughnut Plant, in Grand Street on the Lower East Side, had the very best doughnuts in New York. He told me this while taking my blood pressure. I hadn't mentioned doughnuts. I had been concentrating on breathing slowly in order to lower my blood pressure, although I have no idea if breathing slowly lowers blood pressure.

Advice can often be irritating. I have been told to be less stressed, more than once. Being told to be less stressed automatically raises your level of stress and your blood pressure. Being stressed seems to be the cause of a large number of ailments, not to mention a shorter life expectancy. It is not helpful to know this. It definitely does not help you to be less stressed.

The smallest piece of advice can be surprisingly useful. A few years ago, I was having lunch with a psychiatrist friend – this being New York, it is relatively easy to have a psychiatrist friend – and had just finished giving her a long list of my woes and anxieties.

One of the good things about having a psychiatrist friend is that they are used to listening to complaints. My friend paused for a moment and then gave me one of the most seemingly simple pieces of advice: 'Do more of what makes you happy and less of what stresses you,' she said. I was shocked by the simplicity of that advice. You would think, especially as I was in my mid-sixties, that I might have thought about this option myself, but I hadn't.

Following her advice was a surprisingly difficult thing to do. I did, slowly, start giving myself permission to do more of what makes me happy. My daughter had recently moved from New York to Seattle. I bought airline tickets and flew to Seattle to visit her. Twice in two months.

I also, in the spirit of making myself happier, bought even more pens and pencils. I added them to my already worryingly large collection of pens and pencils. I have loved pens and pencils since I was a child. And, apart from being arrested for shoplifting some pens when I was ten, pens and pencils have always made me happy.

A Dog

After I mistook a fire hydrant on West Broadway for a dog, I felt stupid. As a direct result of the dog that turned out to be a fire hydrant, I went to see my ophthalmologist.

I explained to the ophthalmologist that I had always been wary of dogs, but this dog had seemed harmless. 'It was harmless,' he said to me. 'It was a fire hydrant.' His reply was not helpful. I already knew that the dog was not a dog, it was a fire hydrant.

The ophthalmologist suggested that now might be a good time to have cataract surgery. He had, for three or four years, been telling me that I might, one day, need cataract surgery. The fire hydrant/dog incident seemed to have made the situation more pressing.

Although I knew that cataract surgery was the most common surgical procedure performed in America, I was still nervous. My ophthalmologist recommended an ophthalmic surgeon. He said that this surgeon had done several thousand cataract surgeries.

The ophthalmic surgeon looked like a blonde, blue-eyed teenager. I asked him how old he was. He turned out to be thirty-five. Not a teenager, but still very young. I suggested that he grow some grey hair. 'If you could see properly, you would have noticed that I already have some,' he said. This was a typical New York exchange, direct and semi-humorous.

A few months later, after waving at a tall, large-boned, grey-haired woman who I thought was my husband, I finally made the decision to have my cataracts removed.

Although the post-surgery snack was very disappointing, the surgery itself was, as everyone had told me, quick and painless. Almost overnight, I could see perfectly. I was very excited until I discovered that seeing perfectly had its drawbacks.

When I looked in the mirror, I looked different to myself. For a start, I looked so much paler than I thought I was. I had thought I had quite a sporty look. I don't know why I had seen myself that way. I don't understand the rules or purpose of most sports.

For a week or two after the surgery I had to wear sunglasses, as my eyes were sensitive to light. I had rarely worn sunglasses. In the supermarket, I felt like a former celebrity who hadn't grasped that their fame had faded.

However, I quickly became accustomed to wearing sunglasses. I decided that they made me look more mysterious, more interesting. I began to wear them all the time. Until the night I tripped and fell over some steps outside an old building, on Vandam Street.

My first thought was that the fall had probably ruined my cataract surgery. Then the shock of the fall hit me. I realised that I was lucky to have escaped with just a grazed knee.

I am now used to having good eyesight. Used to being able to see into the distance and across the street, to being able to read without glasses and to knowing that I will never again mistake my husband for a tall, large-boned, grey-haired woman.

I am no longer showing off my vision to anyone who is interested and quite a few others who are not interested. I am also used to having pale skin. And I have never again worn sunglasses at night or in the supermarket.

Intimacy

There is a man who has been part of my life for thirty-three years. We mostly meet in hotel rooms. As soon as he walks through the door, I take off my clothes. I am not prone to throwing off whatever I am wearing. I still have a degree of discomfort about my unclothed body.

Sometimes my husband is with us. Before you start thinking that this is weird, I have to explain that I love this man and he loves me. Our relationship is quite unusual. We are best friends. And he makes all of my clothes. He has made almost everything I have worn for the last three decades.

His name is Graham. Graham Long. He has made my dresses, my coats, my skirts, my shirts, my nighties and my dressing gowns. I should mention that people sometimes mistake my dressing gowns for evening gowns. This is not my fault. It is his fault.

Over the years I have often chosen the fabrics, which is why one of my favourite parts of New York is a relatively drab area formerly known as the Garment District. Spandex House, which sounds as though it sells body-firming undergarments, the sort they used to call girdles, is in the middle of this area. Spandex House sells stretch fabrics.

I love stretch fabrics. They mostly need no ironing and can be squashed into a bag or a suitcase. Spandex House has stretch silk, crepe, cotton or wool. You can also, if you are so inclined, buy stretch metallic spandex, stretch wet-look spandex, and stretch lurex mesh.

The customers are always interesting. There are a lot of gymnasts, dancers, athletes, figure skaters and costume designers. Possibly because of the volume of fabric I have bought, no-one who works there believes me when I say I can't sew. I can't sew. I can't even sew on a button. I mark the spot where the button belongs. I concentrate on every stitch and still the button ends up half a kilometre from where it was supposed to go.

I ship the fabric to whatever country my friend Graham Long is working in – he teaches fashion and design and has worked in India, Vietnam, Taiwan and Australia. Graham has a record of what size I was in what year. I have asked him not to share this information with me. He creates new patterns according to whether my current clothes are snug, which is a common occurrence, or whether they are a comfortable fit.

Graham has also often bought the fabrics. He has bought fabrics I would never have dreamt of buying. He has changed the way I look and he has changed how I see myself.

Although I have sometimes been more adventurous, or possibly misguided, and decided that I could wear gold and silver lamé, Graham has bought fabric in colours I could barely look at. He has bought fabric with wild, floral prints, dizzying, psychedelic patterns and sequined beading.

He is several years younger than me but I think he often forgets that we have grown older. I am now seventy-one. Recently he sent me a dress with glitter inserts. I hadn't thought about glitter since I was a teenager and used to glue it on my face. Now I shed glitter when I walk.

Instead of the subdued greys or blacks I love, I am currently wearing a purple, green, yellow and black swirl of intersecting colours. The fabric is so bright it could be used for traffic lights.

Lexington Avenue

I do not want to be run over by a bus. I have never wanted to be run over by a bus. For many reasons, one of which is I don't want the *New York Times* to refer to the incident as 'An elderly woman was run over by a bus on Lexington Avenue.'

The *New York Times* refers to anyone sixty-five and over as 'elderly'. There are a lot of buses on Lexington Avenue. I often catch a bus on Lexington Avenue. It is not entirely inconceivable that one of the buses may, one day, run over someone. And that someone could be me.

I am not sure what makes sixty-five elderly and sixty-four not yet elderly. In America, everyone who is sixty-five or older is called a senior. The word 'senior', in many contexts, suggests impressive achievement. Senior adviser, senior partner, senior correspondent. Senior, used in terms of being older, has no impressive connotations. It also strongly suggests an imminent expiry date.

I am worried enough about imminent expiry without feeling panicked by the endless information, warnings and advice about old age. This overload of possibly well-intentioned information comes from newspapers, magazines, television, radio and a gazillion online sites.

The *New York Times* has regular articles on aging and how to avoid the pitfalls of aging. One of the most emphasised points is lowering your stress levels. When I read anything about lowering stress levels, my anxiety and my blood pressure soar. If I could lower my stress levels, I would. I am genetically predisposed to be stressed. No-one in my family has ever been accused of being calm.

The *New York Times* also has disquieting articles about preparing for old age. The preparations basically involve spending your youth preparing for your old age. This does not sound like an irresistible proposition.

The AARP – the American Association of Retired People – tackles subjects like financial health, thrift tips, help buttons and easy-to-use flip phones. I know that all of this is useful but I find it mildly depressing.

There are articles on funeral preparations – the headline of the latest one was 'Don't Delay, Plan Today'. I only read about the funeral preparations because this article had been preceded by the fact that one in three seniors will fall this year and that every eleven seconds an older adult is treated for a fall. Reading about funeral preparations seemed relatively peaceful after the falls, the flip phones and the thrift tips.

Age has been a problem for me in my writing. I have, several times, tried to make the main female character in my novels the same age as I was. This has never worked. Regardless of whether I was forty-five, fifty-four or sixty-five, I always dropped several years off her age. Making her my age somehow made her feel too old.

In the novel I am currently writing she is called Nellie Nathan. I have changed Nellie Nathan's age ten or twelve times until it has felt just right. She is sixty-nine. I am seventy-one.

When I was in my twenties and thirties, I had a fantasy of spending my old age relaxing in a deck chair, in the sun, eating chocolate. This definitely turned out to be a fantasy. Firstly, I no longer like being in the sun. And secondly, who eats chocolate in the sun? Chocolate was never meant to be eaten in the heat. It melts, changes shape and never tastes the same again.

Contradictions

New Yorkers almost always look purposeful. Everyone seems to be on their way somewhere or in the middle of something. We don't stroll, we stride. The only people pausing or strolling are tourists.

New Yorkers can order their take-out breakfast or lunch with breathtaking speed. This event usually takes place in a deli, and should be a major tourist attraction – if not an Olympic event.

I like the egalitarian nature of delis. Last week I had lunch at a deli on 59th Street in Midtown Manhattan. The deli is close to my dermatologist and my dental surgeon – a consequence of aging is that you spend much more time with doctors, dentists, podiatrists and physiotherapists.

Most delis have a salad bar with a large number of ingredients to choose from. I rehearsed what I wanted in my salad so I wouldn't hold up the others in the queue.

The man in front of me ordered his salad ingredients at the speed of light. He ordered bacon, salami, fried chicken, boiled eggs and lettuce. I'm not sure men understand salads.

With all of this emphasis on speed and everyone in a rush, you'd think New Yorkers have no time for slower sentiments like nostalgia. But, New York is a city of contradictions. There is something to contradict everything.

You would be surprised at what brings us to a standstill. And it's not just salads made of bacon, salami and fried chicken. It is nostalgia. The legendary late New York columnist, Pete Hamill, called nostalgia 'the most powerful of New York emotions'.

Roz Chast, the *New Yorker* cartoonist, said in her latest book, 'I try not to freak out every time a favourite restaurant or bookstore closes. I remind myself that life is change and that life in New York is definitely change.'

I don't like change. I would like the world to stay the same – except for more equal opportunities, more advances in medicine – the continuing presence of iPhones, iPads and Caffe Roma, which is a ten-minute walk from where I live.

Many of us who live in this city have intimate relationships with our local cafes, bookstores, restaurants, drycleaners and corner stores. It is almost like the intimacy between old friends. Or, in some cases, old acquaintances.

When Milady's, a very old fashioned, slightly run-down pub in SoHo closed, I missed it even though I had only been there once in the over twenty-five years I lived in SoHo. I liked knowing Milady's was there, and had been there for a long time.

And I was distraught for months after Caffe Dante, in MacDougal Street, closed. I used to go there almost every afternoon. The staff and the regulars felt like family. We knew a lot about each other.

I feel nostalgic more frequently than I did when I was young. I often find myself wistfully thinking about the time when my children were small. We went on vacations and outings together, we travelled together, we ate our meals together. It all seemed so cosy. And simple.

My children are now dispersed in different cities in different states. They have jobs, partners and their own children. It takes dozens of phone calls and emails and long-term planning to get us all together.

I sometimes try to make them feel guilty about living so far from me, but it doesn't work. They just suggest that I live closer to them. But it took me years to get used to New York. Used to the noise, used to the traffic, and used to the speed and the rush. I can't leave now.

A Toilet

A neighbour I barely knew told me she had a new toilet.
I had hardly ever spoken to this woman. I didn't even know
her name. We were standing in the lobby of the building
and she was talking to me about her toilet. It is not as
though toilets are a popular topic of conversation among
New Yorkers.

My neighbour looked very excited about her toilet.
Apparently it was similar to a Japanese bidet toilet. In brief,
this toilet sprayed the relevant parts of your anatomy with
warm water or, if you were partial to hot, cold or tepid water,
you could adjust the temperature. When you were done with
the spraying, which could last for two or three minutes, or
possibly a whole day, depending on your preference, the
toilet dried those body parts with an air dryer.

This was already a lot to know about someone you
have never spoken to. But there was more. The toilet,

the neighbour explained to me, also deodorised and automatically cleaned inside and outside before and after each use. I assumed that the deodorising and the automatic cleaning and drying inside and outside referred to the toilet and not the body parts, which had already had their share of cleaning and drying.

I thanked her and started to leave but she followed me to let me know that the toilet had an inbuilt night-light. I didn't want to even start thinking about why you would want or need a night-light in your toilet.

She lowered her voice, and said, 'As we get older, it can be increasingly harder to clean up after using the toilet.'

I could feel that whatever spring was left in my step was sagging. I had to leave. I fled. I think she might have still been talking. I tried to not think about the increasing difficulty of, as my nameless neighbour put it, cleaning yourself up after using the toilet.

When I was young, my father used to call the toilet 'The only place where the Queen walks with her own feet.'

This puzzled me for ages. I wondered how the Queen could walk without her own feet and how the Queen could walk with someone else's feet. I finally asked my father whose feet the Queen used when she walked to other locations. He explained that the Queen was carried everywhere else on her own throne, which he always pronounced drone. Today being carried by your own drone might not seem as far-fetched as being carried on a throne.

In one of my non-fiction books, I wrote about my father reading his detective books in the toilet. I added a few more details and then worried that those details would bother my father. I consulted with my husband and my three adult children. They all agreed that my father would not be at all bothered.

My father called me after he had read that non-fiction book. He said that he cried when he was reading it. I felt sick. I knew I shouldn't have written about my father and the toilet. I asked him what had made him cry. He said that he had never realised that I had suffered at all when I was growing up. He said he should have paid more attention. That he should not have thought that because I hadn't been imprisoned in a Nazi death camp, I had never been in pain. By this time, I was crying so much I could hardly speak.

I didn't think that writing about my weight and my anxiety and my analysts would bother him. I had written about those things before, but perhaps not in as much detail. I kept apologising. My father said that it was a very good thing that he now understood more about that part of my life. It took me years to understand exactly how extraordinary my father's response was.

I learned a lot from my father. And I am not talking about the Queen and her throne. One day I was complaining about some guests who were planning to stay with us when they came to New York. I didn't dislike these people, but I didn't like them – there is a fine distinction between not disliking and not liking. I complained that the loft we were then living in was a fairly open space. It may have been large but there was very little privacy. We only ever had friends we loved stay there with us. This is the short version of the long conversation my father and I had about these potential guests.

My father ended the discussion. 'If there is room in your heart, there is room in your home,' he said. I felt terrible. I felt worse when he added, 'And you have three toilets.'

Nothing Wrong

My mother used to say that if you woke up in the morning and there was nothing wrong with you, you must be dead. It used to make me laugh. I think the truth is more likely to be that if you wake up in the morning and there is nothing wrong, you must be young.

Recently, in one week, I had appointments with my dermatologist, a vascular surgeon, a dental surgeon and my ophthalmologist. The appointment with the dental surgeon was in order to have the last of several dental implants. Not only is this surgery not exactly a picnic, it is, in New York, outrageously expensive. I will have to live to at least one hundred and ten to justify the expense, I said to the dental surgeon.

I started worrying about dying in the next week or in the next year. If I tripped and fell down a set of stairs, or was knocked over by one of the many bicycle messengers, particularly in Downtown Manhattan where I live – who seem to ride at high speed and the wrong way down the many, narrow, one-way streets – it would be a terrible waste of money.

Money I could have invested in something that I could have left to my children. You can't bequeath dental implants. No-one wants used teeth.

After a few weeks of clinging anxiously to the handrail of any stairs I used and not crossing streets against the lights – something all New Yorkers do – I started to feel as though I was ninety-two not seventy-two. Being seventy-two already felt old enough, I didn't want to feel ninety-two. I wanted to experience something exciting.

I thought about organising a trip to Vietnam as a surprise birthday present for my husband's seventy-second birthday. That would not have been easy. I am not a good liar. I look shifty and guilty before the lie has even come out of mouth.

In order to stop thinking about whether I could lie to my husband, I decided to buy tickets to a Bob Dylan concert. I bought the tickets to the Bob Dylan concert not because I love Bob Dylan, although I have nothing against him. I bought the tickets because my husband loves Bob Dylan. He loves Bob Dylan just a little bit less than he loves me.

The concert was at the Beacon Theatre, one of New York's most beautiful theatres. The audience comprised mostly people in their sixties, seventies and eighties. They all looked as though they were overjoyed to be there. No-one screamed, but there were roars of applause, the loudest of which seemed to come from my husband.

At one point, Bob Dylan, who had been playing the piano and singing, stood up, walked to the centre of the stage and sang. The audience burst into sounds of sheer joy. A joy that was tinged with a sense of relief that their now 77-year-old idol could still stand and sing. It felt like the sort of relief that some of us feel when we see that we can still walk at a reasonable speed or are still able to feel overly excited when we are considerably older than we used to be.

A few months later, I looked up the vaccinations necessary for travel to Vietnam. And then I booked airline tickets to Hanoi.

Bomb Cyclone

I am so sick of snow. I used to think snow was exciting. Now I glare at snowflakes. I know they don't notice. Last winter we had a bomb cyclone. There were warnings that this bomb cyclone was on the way. The warnings, especially on television, were delivered with a sense of urgency.

I feel very wary about anything that contains the word 'bomb'. Even 'bombshell', when used to describe a woman, bothers me. The official term for a bomb cyclone is 'explosive cyclogenesis'. Unless you are a scientist, it is not worth trying to understand what that means. However, it seems to be clear that it would be best, if possible, to avoid an explosive cyclogenesis.

In America, the weather report often sounds alarming. The climate is so varied that something bothering is always happening somewhere. I panic at weather forecasts. I fret about strong winds expected in Indianapolis or

Albuquerque and wonder if they will reach New York. This is when it would be handy to be able to read maps. I have no idea how far Albuquerque or Indianapolis – or Vancouver, Portland, Salt Lake City, San Antonio or San Diego – are from New York.

I have never been able to read maps. Maps of the world don't help me locate countries or continents. And road maps make me feel even more lost. For people like me, GPS systems are a gift from God.

The bomb cyclone was predicted to bring very strong winds and over twelve inches of snow. Strong winds and snow are, I have learned from my thirty years in New York, not a good combination.

I decided, for no logical reason, to go to Shelter Island, a small island, ninety miles from New York City. This decision was truly illogical, if not stupid. The weather on Shelter Island, in winter, is usually much worse than it is in New York City.

My husband, who is very easygoing, went along with my plan to go to Shelter Island. I feel very lucky to have an easygoing husband, although, as my daughter has unnecessarily pointed out, compared to me, most people look easygoing.

In New York, bad weather rarely causes power outages. On Shelter Island, bad weather is much more likely to result in no power. No power means no heat, no stove, no oven, no microwave and often no water. By the time I thought about that, it was too late. We were on our way.

On Shelter Island, I decided to prepare for the bomb cyclone. I found four flashlights and bought another six. I had twenty spare batteries lined up on the kitchen bench. The flashlights were not small. They were designed to light a large tent. I also filled the bath and several restaurant-sized saucepans with water. I precooked food which would taste fine unheated. And after that I felt calm.

We were really pounded by the bomb cyclone. The door to the driveway of the house was blocked by about three feet of snow on either side and the driveway itself was inaccessible. We had to be plowed out by a rather large plow truck.

But, guess what? We didn't have a power outage. What I learned from this experience was that although I was well prepared, I could have done better. For the next bomb cyclone or polar vortex I plan to also have a portable iPhone charger and a battery-operated gadget that heats up coffee.

A Conversation

I was walking along Grand Street on my way to the East River. I love the East River. It never seems to be crowded although there are bike paths, walking paths and beautiful seating areas. I was walking right behind two women in their sixties who looked as though they were close friends. I was trying to pass them when I heard one of them say to the other, 'Do you masturbate?'

'Myself or others?' her friend replied.

I came to an almost abrupt stop. I was desperate to hear the rest of the conversation. I tried to look casual. How often do you overhear a conversation like that? Women seem to be reticent to talk about their genitals.

Who were the 'others' the friend was referring to? And how many of them were there? By this time, I had passed the two women. I wanted to turn back and follow the women or ask them if I could join the conversation.

I didn't. I think I was scared. Scared of seeming weird or friendless.

It was hard to stop thinking about that masturbation conversation. I hardly noticed the river. I could have been walking in the Mojave Desert or in a deserted area in an undesirable neighbourhood, my brain was preoccupied with masturbation. The two women on Grand Street had sounded as casual as though they were having a conversation about the weather.

I think I have talked about the weather with just about everyone I know as well as perfect strangers. Not many women I know have ever brought up the subject of masturbating themselves. And neither have I.

My father was never shy about talking about sex. Years after my mother died, my father had a relationship with a woman he described, after spending the night with her, as 'very energetic'. In case I hadn't quite understood, he looked me straight in the eye and with a very knowing look repeated, '*very* energetic'.

I was a bit horrified that my father was sharing this information with me. And then I started picturing this particular 86-year-old woman hanging from a chandelier or standing on her head or doing the rhumba while having sex with my father. I tried, unsuccessfully, to get these images out of my head.

I can't stand on my head or do the rhumba. I have never

been athletic. At my very competitive Melbourne high school, sport was, for my class, a compulsory subject. We had to walk, and turn, and sometimes do the splits on a balance beam, an elevated, narrow plank of wood or some other hard surface.

Why? Why did we have to do this? How much of your life are you going to spend walking on an elevated narrow plank? And why was it deemed necessary to be able do the splits? I thought we were at this school to become the world's best scientists, doctors, economists or philosophers.

We also had to leap over something called a vaulting horse. Maybe if you had aspirations to be a detective or a spy, being able to leap could be useful. I never could leap over that vaulting horse. I had trouble leaping over a puddle.

Being a detective or a spy or a gymnast or a ballerina was not in my future. My mother, in a moment of misguided optimism, enrolled me in ballet classes at a local dance school. Ballet school exhausted me. It was a series of mishaps, disasters and humiliating incidents.

I was a bit chunky. The largest-sized tutu almost strangled me. I bumped into other dancers and ruined their *adagios* and *arabesques*. I threw myself into a *pirouette* and landed on the floor. Not long after that, I left – or maybe I was asked to leave. 'Lily had a problem with ballet,' the teacher explained to the class as I was leaving.

At the moment I am having a problem. The problem has nothing to do with ballet. I am typing the word 'lust' instead of 'list'. This is not intentional. I discovered that I use the word list with alarming frequency. In the last few weeks I have, in emails, said, 'can you lust', 'I am lusting', 'this lust is driving me crazy' and 'Do you have the lust I sent you?'

I have, several times, apologised, saying that I meant to write 'list' not 'lust'.

While I was dealing with all this lust, I read that Chopin, who moved from Poland to Paris when he was about twenty, was rumoured to have had an affair with Countess Delfina Potocka, a great beauty and a fine singer. Countess Delfina Potocka, who sang to Chopin on his deathbed, had what one of Chopin's biographers described as a 'notoriously hospitable vulva.'

I was overawed by the power of those three words. I mean, how often do you hear such an intriguing, if not electrifying, description of a vulva?

I have my own small history with Chopin. In the early 1980s I travelled with my husband to Poland, to Lodz, where both of my parents were born. I had never seen the country where my parents' lives had a normality, where they lived with their parents and siblings, went to school, studied, had aunts and uncles and cousins, had friends and made plans for the future.

A future that was hijacked and stripped of every aspect of normality.

We hired a guide, Mrs Potoki-Okolska. We were driving from Warsaw to Lodz. Mrs Potoki-Okolska was a formidable woman. She had firm opinions on everything, including whether it was okay to open the window of a very overheated car in winter. It wasn't.

My father had drawn a map of Lodz for me in a school exercise book. He had marked the street address of his family's apartment block. My father, the youngest child, lived in the top apartment with his mother and father. His much older siblings had had their own apartments in the building. My father had also marked the small apartment in a far less salubrious area where my mother and her seven siblings were raised.

We were counting on Mrs Potoki-Okolska being able to get us into my father's and mother's former homes.

Suddenly, Mrs Potoki-Okolska announced we were stopping. We were at Żelazowa Wola. I felt my almost combustible combination of anxiety, excitement and fear rising. I just wanted to get to Lodz.

'I don't want to stop,' I said.

'This is Chopin's home,' she said in a semi-militaristic tone before almost dragging me out of the car.

We looked at Chopin's house, Chopin's piano and Chopin's mother's piano – Chopin's mother was a piano teacher. We saw Chopin's bedroom and Chopin's mother's bedroom, Chopin's bathroom and Chopin's garden. Just as I thought we were about to leave, Mrs Potoki-Okolska said we must see Chopin's desk and Chopin's table.

Eventually, Mrs Potoki-Okolska reluctantly left Żelazowa Wola, humming *La Polonaise*. While Mrs Potoki-Okolska was humming, everything in my brain was blurring. I couldn't have told you anything about the pianos, the garden, the bathroom or the bedrooms. They all merged and meshed together in my head.

I do remember Mrs Potoki-Okolska saying that Chopin was shy and that he preferred to play the piano in the dark. She said that when he played at small gatherings he would ask to have the lights extinguished. Mrs Potoki-Okolska also told me that Chopin's last words were, 'Mother, my poor mother.' I thought about that for years.

In Lodz, Mrs Potoki-Okolska was a force of nature.

She got us into the apartment building my father, his siblings and parents lived in and owned. This was no mean feat. Poland was still under communist rule and the conditions were grim. Mrs Potoki-Okolska knocked on every door in the building. She jammed her foot in the doorway the minute anyone opened their door.

She planted her foot firmly inside the door of the apartment on the top floor where my father lived with his mother and father. She persuaded the man who opened the door to let us into the apartment. It was one of the most emotional days of my life. And would change my life.

I said goodbye to Mrs Potoki-Okolska. I hugged her and kissed her and cried. She told me I should remember that Chopin played the piano in the dark all of his life, and that he only gave about thirty public concerts in his lifetime.

I thought about Mrs Potoki-Okolska the day I read about Countess Delfina Potocka. I thought Mrs Potoki-Okolska might have been quite pleased to hear about Countess Delfina Potocka singing to Chopin on his deathbed. But I am not sure how she would have felt about the Countess's notoriously hospitable vulva.

I decided that I really had to stop thinking about Countess Delfina Potocka. I didn't want to derail myself by thinking about my vulva and whether it was hospitable enough.

Pets

I know, and have read many times, that having pets is supposed to lower your stress and extend your longevity. I have always found it stressful to have pets. This has probably lessened any possibility I might have had of living to one hundred and has possibly increased my chances of being run over by a horse-drawn cart, tomorrow. Yes, there are horses and carts in Manhattan, mostly in the Central Park area.

I have, however, found that having a pet does make a difference to my levels of stress. My stress level seems to be permanently set on high. Having a pet shifts my stress level from high to sky high.

When my children were not yet adults, we had a series of pet disasters. A canary called Flutter was killed by a butcherbird, who prised open Flutter's cage and dispensed with Flutter. Flutter was replaced with Flutter II. And then Flutter II was replaced by Flutter III. Not one of the Flutters died of natural causes.

My son's pet guinea pig fell off a tree while my son, who was three, was trying to teach the guinea pig how to balance on a branch. Rigor mortis had already set in before the deceased guinea pig was discovered.

Two cats went missing and a sheep was, mysteriously, stolen from our backyard, when we lived in Australia. Why we had a sheep in our backyard is a long story. We also had a dog. The dog was loved by my children and my husband. His name was Solly. Solly had a penchant for digging under a fence and running away. Solly had a tag engraved with his name and our phone number.

At least three or four times a week, I received calls telling me that someone had found Solly. Every caller called Solly 'Dolly'. The engraving on Solly's tag must have been a bit blurry. Each time, I spent fifteen to twenty minutes explaining that it was Solly, not Dolly, and that I knew Solly well enough to know Solly would come home.

One of the callers threatened to report me to the Royal Society for the Prevention of Cruelty to Animals. That sort of threat is highly unlikely to be made to New York dog owners. New Yorkers are, on the whole, devoted to their dogs. They seem to think of every aspect of their dog's physical, social and emotional needs.

Many dog owners in New York City employ dog walkers to walk their dogs once or twice a day. If the dog doesn't seem satisfied with that, there is another option. They can have their dogs picked up and taken for three- or four-hour hikes in the countryside. Some dogs get to go on hikes two or three times a week. Companies such as My Dog Hikes are doing well.

The dogs are not just taken to any old, boring piece of countryside, they are taken to beautiful state parks and nature reserves, with hiking trails and hilly terrain.

All of these dog owners are probably going to live until they are a hundred and ten. Not me. Anyway, I am seventy-two. At this stage, ninety-two seems good enough, to me.

Food

My husband loves food. In New York you have a huge range of food choices. You can't walk a block without passing something or somewhere to eat.

For breakfast, while I am eating high-fibre cereal and fat-free yoghurt, my husband is often out having eggs, cheese, bacon and a spicy sauce on a brioche roll, or else picking up what our local bagel store calls a 'Classic New York Bagel'. This is a sesame-seed bagel filled with sliced, smoked, Nova Scotia salmon, cream cheese, tomato, onion, capers and dill.

My husband is an adventurous eater. He will try anything. He loved the spinal-cord soup he had in a small Mexican restaurant. The spinal cords of pigs and cows, I now know, look very much like noodles. I was fine when I thought he was eating a bowl of soup with noodles. When I found out that the noodles were not noodles, I couldn't finish my grilled-chicken-breast salad.

And I have to look away when he eats three or four bull's head tacos. The bull's head tacos contain parts of the bull's eyes, brains and tongue. The tacos are not small. I am not sure whether it is the volume of the food my husband can eat or the content that bothers me most.

My husband has never counted a calorie in his life. He was trim when he was twenty-two and he is still trim at seventy-two. I have an encyclopedic knowledge of calories. I can add up calories faster than the speed of light. I can also tell you the difference in calories between an apple and a pear. Or an orange and a grapefruit. I am probably the only person I know who is impressed by that ability.

My husband has also never been on a diet. He has never thought about or planned a diet. I spent my high-school years calculating how many weeks it would take me to lose ten or fifteen pounds. My high-school notebooks were filled with calorie calculations. There was no room left for algebra or trigonometry.

I love my husband. I left another husband for this husband, almost forty years ago. But sometimes, when I am eating steamed broccoli or I am in a state of shock because I have just inadvertently eaten four thick slices of bread, I look at my husband and think this is so unfair.

One day, preferably before I am one hundred and one, I hope to eat kilos of cheesecake and maybe a few slices of very dense chocolate cake. I hope I won't be eating grilled, skinless chicken and steamed green beans.

At the moment, I am sitting in my New York apartment eating my breakfast of high-fibre cereal and fat-free yoghurt.

Cities

I have only ever lived in cities. I have never lived anywhere that has too many trees or shrubs. I love cities.

I like living among a lot of people. New York City, the city I have lived in for the last thirty years, can feel a little crowded. But then I remind myself that I like crowded streets – I feel as though their lifeforce is contagious.

I think that cities have limitless options and possibilities. Although sometimes I have been forced to see some of the limitations of city life.

When I was young, I lived in London for two years. In Baker Street. Where the legendary, although fictitious, Sherlock Holmes lived. I was seven months pregnant with my son. One day I saw an advertisement seeking a home for a baby bear.

I have always liked bears. Not that I have ever been closer to a bear than three or four hundred feet.

And that particular bear was sound asleep, in a zoo.

I called the owner of the baby bear. We had several excited conversations about bears. The relationship faltered a bit when I asked how tall the bear would be when it was fully grown. The answer was six feet. I then had to explain that our ceilings were not very high.

'You live in a house?' he said. 'Oh, no,' I replied. 'I live in an apartment, in Baker Street. It has two bedrooms.' The relationship between me and the owner of the baby bear went downhill after that. In fact, it came to an abrupt end.

By this time, I was eight months pregnant. I had never held a baby, bathed a baby or fed a baby. I was not particularly worried about that. I was focused on not thinking about an image I had seen in a movie. The image was of a woman screaming and sweating while she gave birth.

I had forgotten to think about the fact that I would, after the birth, have to take the baby home with me. I don't know how I managed to overlook that. My son slept in a bucket for the first two weeks of his life. It was quite a spacious, purple bucket, although, on reflection, a drawer might have been even better.

Spending the first two weeks of his life in a bucket doesn't seem to have affected my son. He is a doctor and has four children, none of whom has ever slept in a bucket.

My son has never mentioned the bucket. He does know that it was spacious and purple. But he has never complained about it or even thought it was strange. He has, however, mentioned, more than once, that he can't believe I sent him to a school that didn't teach Latin.

Latin? I have hardly ever thought about Latin. I have thought about Latin even less than I thought about the fact that that I had to bring him home from hospital with me. Who thinks about Latin? Especially when your child is five or six. Or maybe even nine or ten.

An advantage of being older is that I no longer feel bad about the Latin and I would now never even think about living with a baby bear. I am, however, still pleased that the bucket was a particularly nice shade of purple.

Funerals

For the last few years, I have been thinking about funerals. Well, mostly my own funeral. It is not that I plan on dying soon, but I do think it is best, if possible, to plan everything ahead of time, including meals, diets, travel, conversations and funerals.

I have prepared a list of people who I definitely don't want at my funeral. I have told my husband, more than once, that I will be furious if anyone on the list turns up at my funeral. I know that I have overlooked the fact that it could be hard to be furious when you are dead.

Last year, I went to a funeral during which, if you listened to the speeches, you would not have known that the deceased, Henry, a writer, was an extraordinarily articulate, witty and almost mesmerisingly clever man. 'If Henry were here, he would have walked out of this funeral,' I said to a friend who was sitting next to me.

My friend agreed. Unfortunately, Henry was in the coffin.

The more I have thought about my funeral, the more certain I have become that it would be best if I could be at my own funeral. And not in a coffin. My list of people who would be banned from my funeral would remain the same and I would be there to make sure that not one of them slipped in.

I think we should all be at our own funerals. That way we would be able to hear the mostly wonderful things people say about us and we could correct the speakers who get some detail wrong. Also, why deprive yourself of the chance to hear how much people love you and how much they will miss you?

You would be able to see their pain and their distress. You would be able to see who cried and who did not and, more importantly, who didn't turn up. You could also make a speech yourself, which I think would be a big bonus.

You would miss out on all of this if you waited until you died.

I live on the Lower East Side, on the border of New York's Chinatown. A few days ago, there was a funeral at the Chinese funeral parlour on the corner of Canal and Ludlow streets. There were Buddhist priests in long, black robes, musicians playing trumpets and drums and a stunningly beautiful array of flowers on top of the hearse and on elevated frames, on the pavement. A dignified procession of hundreds of people, in groups and with linked arms, walked slowly down Ludlow Street.

I wondered if the person who had died knew how many people had cried and looked heartbroken, and if the person knew that parts of Ludlow and Henry Streets had been closed to traffic – street closings, in New York, are usually reserved for presidents and other heads of state.

When I got home, I started thinking about what would be an appropriate outfit for me to wear to my funeral. And what food I should serve after the service.

I think a large poppyseed cake, the sort that is ninety per cent poppyseed and ten per cent cake, would be perfect. Well, perfect for me. There is a small hitch. The best poppyseed cake I have ever had was from Thoben Bakery, in Berlin. Then I realise that my friend, Johanna, who lives in Berlin, would definitely come to my funeral. She could fly over with a whole tray of the cake.

As for what to wear, I decided to wear black. I often wear black. Wearing black at a funeral suggests a certain solemnity. And I definitely don't want to look overly-cheerful at my own funeral.

Aging

Geoffrey, who has cut my hair for thirty years, told me that I was his only client over forty who had never had any work done to her face.

By 'work', Geoffrey meant plastic surgery. I was feeling quite pleased with myself as it seemed that not having had any work done on my face was a good thing, until Geoffrey added, 'Well, you could do with a little lift here and maybe a small tuck here,' as he pointed somewhere in the vicinity of my mouth.

I stopped listening. I didn't want to hear what else I could do with. I could definitely do with a greater grip on basic geography and an ability to sing in tune or to be trilingual. But plastic surgery? No, you can count me out.

Cosmetic procedures and surgeries are on the rise. Everyone wants to look younger. Even thirty-year-olds. A whole wave of beauty bars have opened in New York.

Beauty bars are places where you can have injections of fillers and botox during your lunch break.

I didn't know what fillers were. Fillers, a friend explained to me, are an injection of soft-tissue filler into the skin to fill in facial wrinkles. That did not sound appealing, to me.

How to look younger has been a staple subject in magazines and newspapers for decades, if not centuries. These articles used to be aimed solely at women. Now losing your looks, looking older, has become a common concern for men as well as women.

Men are having their chins reshaped and their jaws reconstructed. Soon, many of us will no longer look like ourselves or even a close relative of who we used to be.

I have never once thought about losing my looks. There is so much else to lose. The list of possible losses is frightening. And I am not talking about keys or iPhones.

I am also a coward. The thought of lifts and tucks and botox and fillers fills me with dread and, apart from that, I am more superstitious than I like to admit. I think that if I even thought about having plastic surgery, I might jinx myself and fall, break my hip or fracture my ribs and puncture my lungs, which would require surgery of a different sort.

Maybe having started off with what were considered not the right sort of looks has helped me to not think about losing my looks. I was chubby as a teenager and grew larger in my twenties. In high school, I didn't seem to attract many, if not any, boys.

At fifteen, I decided that if my looks were not going to attract boys, I would have to be interesting. Very interesting. I saw several Ingmar Bergman movies and I started reading about existentialism.

I am not sure that I understood exactly what existentialism was, but I managed to drop the word 'existentialism' into almost every conversation I had in high school that year. There was no response. It was as though I had inadvertently started speaking in Russian.

I talked about Ingmar Bergman to a boy I met at a local dance. And then introduced the subject of existentialism. He fled in the opposite direction the minute the dance ended. A similar thing happened with two other boys. I gave up. Existentialism clearly wasn't working for me.

I decided on a different approach. I would ditch existentialism and buy a bright pink lipstick that would match my new, bright pink skirt.

Information

A 93-year-old woman came into my favourite stationery store, Stevdan, on Sixth Avenue. I know the woman was ninety-three because she told the cashier. She was, she also said, looking for a 2017 diary. 'A large one with a whole page for each day,' she added. We were still less than halfway through 2016.

I watched her look through several 2017 diaries. I was mesmerised. Mesmerised by her confidence that not only would she still be around, but she would be very busy. She clearly had a lot of plans.

I have a lot of trouble making long-term plans. And it is not because I am now seventy. I was like that at forty. I feel as though I am tempting fate, pushing my luck, if I make plans that are more than a few months into the future.

It doesn't help that I subscribe to an email newsletter called WebMD. Do not subscribe to this. Every day

I receive an email with subject headings like 'Nasty Infections You Never Want To Get' or 'Surprising Ways To Hurt Your Liver' or 'Could You Be Anemic And Not Know It?' or 'Should You Worry If Your Heart Skips A Beat?' This had a subheading of 'That is a warning sign of atrial fibrillation.'

I tried hard not to panic at the thought of atrial fibrillation. Surely everyone's heart occasionally missed a beat? I marked that email as being unread and planned to later read how to manage atrial fibrillation, should it strike me.

'The Best And Worst Foods For Sleep' was more alluring. I am a terrible sleeper. If you are too, it appears that warm milk, bananas and honey are good for a good night's sleep. Hamburgers and chocolate are not. I couldn't really see myself sitting in bed at night eating a hamburger. Some chocolate, maybe.

I was in the dentist's waiting room when the subject of that day's WebMD email was 'Is There A Right And Wrong Way To Poop?' Apparently there is. How could you resist an email like that? You may have been, as WebMD put it, pooping the wrong way for decades.

A woman sitting next to me glanced at my iPhone. 'I subscribe to WebMD, too,' she said. I nodded. I didn't say anything. I didn't want to pursue the subject of pooping. Not in the dentist's waiting room, anyway.

New Yorkers share surprisingly intimate information. Information is currency in this city. Information about anything. Information about real estate, divorce laws, your dog's diet, your partner's irritating or strange habits.

In a cheese shop, a Catholic priest once told me how to cook pasta for thirty priests. I was fascinated, even though I thought it was highly unlikely to be a piece of information that would come in handy one day.

I put my iPhone in my bag, picked up a magazine and nodded, again, at my fellow subscriber to WebMD. She wasn't deterred. 'I just bought a Squatty Potty,' she said. A Squatty Potty? I didn't even want to ask what a Squatty Potty was. Luckily, the dentist called her in.

I googled Squatty Potty. It is a stool that fits around the base of the toilet, elevates your legs into a squatting position and, as the ad said, 'Opens and unkinks your colon'. Before I had left the dentist's, I had ordered one.

A Cruelty Quotient

I was thrilled to read in the *New York Times* that sales of lace push-up bras, high-cut panties, low-cut bras, sheer-back Brazilian panties and crotchless panties had soared in the US. Fleur du Mal, a company known for its lingerie, had apparently sold out of four styles of their crotchless panties.

I have never understood crotchless panties. Did wearing them mean you were always ready to have sex? Whatever it meant, I was happy that sales of lace bras and crotchless panties had soared. Purchases of these racy undergarments started rising dramatically in March.

I am a bit loath to admit this, but in March I wasn't buying sheer-back panties or low-cut lace bras. I was buying beans. I bought bags of beans. Pinto beans, lima beans, black beans and chickpeas and lentils. I also bought diced, dried vegetables, dried potato flakes, onion flakes and garlic flakes, forty cans of organic tomatoes, fifty cartons of salt-reduced chicken stock, a sack of rice and a three-kilo bucket of oats.

Why did I buy a three-kilo bucket of oats? I have no idea. I hardly ever eat oats, and it would take my husband several decades to get through three kilos of oats.

I think I just panicked. The first cases of the coronavirus had arrived in the US in late February. I am prone to panic. My husband isn't. He lacks a panic gene. I have to do the panicking for both of us.

Not too long after that we were in the middle of a pandemic. When the coronavirus hit New York, it hit with a vengeance. The virus roared through the city. So many people were ill and so many people were dying. Bodies were being carried out of hospitals in black plastic bags.

You could feel the pain and suffering in the air. Both of my parents were imprisoned in Nazi ghettos and death camps. I grew up in the middle of much pain and suffering. What was happening now felt frighteningly familiar.

To add to this pain, we have the tragedy of having a president who is a heartless, hateful narcissist. Trump has a cruelty quotient that would be admired by the world's greatest dictators, past and present.

Trump's principles are simple. Always blame someone else. Keep blaming them. Lie about everything. Keep repeating that lie. Be as uninformed as possible. And believe that you are the best, the best ever, regardless of the subject.

Trump could say that he had danced the role of Albrecht in the Dutch National Ballet's production of *Giselle* and he would believe that he had. He would not be able to resist adding that no-one in the history of ballet had ever danced the demanding *pas de deux* in the second act as brilliantly as he had. And he would believe that.

While the virus is spreading in several states, Trump states that the virus is not dangerous. He says that it will just magically disappear. Hospitals are already overcrowded and ill-equipped.

My son is an emergency-room doctor. I admire him and I fear for him. He seems relatively calm. I am not relatively anxious. I am *very* anxious. I occasionally wish he was an accountant.

Weeks later, while still denying the lethal nature of the virus, Trump suggests that if we inject or ingest a common household disinfectant it could 'knock the virus out in a minute, in one minute'. Doctors rush to warn people of the dire consequences of injecting or drinking these caustic chemicals.

Trump has already mused about killing the virus by hitting the body 'with a tremendous amount of light'. 'You have to bring the light inside the body through the skin or in some other way,' he said.

This sounds like a circus, doesn't it?

The internet is overflowing with hilarious and often brilliant parodies of Trump. There are caricatures, satires, comedy skits about Trump. We send them to each other and laugh and laugh. It feels so good to laugh. Meanwhile, Trump keeps his focus on revenge and destruction.

I start focusing on my need to have a haircut. I become obsessed with my need to have a haircut. My hair looks messy and unkempt. And not in a good way. New York is in lockdown. All hair salons and barber shops are shut. I start wearing my hair pulled back in a bun. I feel like a headmistress. Most of us haven't been able to have a haircut for months. Suddenly, men who are hedge-fund managers or investment bankers look like sensitive poets. It is very disconcerting.

I skype with my friend, Ginny, regularly. We have an unspoken agreement to *not* mention Trump. We talk about regular things. We talk about each other, we talk about our children, we talk about the past and the future. All without mentioning Trump. It is such a relief. It makes everything feel more normal.

I become transfixed by Trump's twitch. I have noticed this twitch before. Now I am fixated by it. Watching the twitch is so much less distressing than listening to what Trump is saying.

The twitch is a short, sharp, upward and backward twist of his left shoulder. This twitch mostly occurs when Trump lowers his voice in an attempt to project some sincerity as he slowly reads from notes someone else has written for him. The twitch looks almost like an allergic response to anything that could contain a fact.

Before becoming bewitched by the twitch, I was starting to feel numb, almost inured to the daily onslaught of Trump's threats and menace. I felt dazed. Unable to think. 'Trump has drained my brain,' I said to my husband.

After the video of the shocking murder of George Floyd by the police becomes public, the Black Lives Matter movement gains more momentum than it ever has. So many people are enraged. And so many people finally grasp the huge numbers of Black men who have been and continue to be murdered by police.

There are protests all over the US – and in other parts of the world. The protesters are men and women, old, young and middle-aged. There are Black, brown and white people. There are so many of them. They are united and they march together.

For the first time in decades it feels as though real change – substantial change – is possible. Hundreds of thousands of people are protesting against inequality and injustice. There is an outrage that crosses generational, racial and cultural borders.

So many of us feel hopeful. Hopeful that there will be a long overdue overhaul of healthcare, education, childcare and the justice system. Hopeful that racism and discrimination will diminish. For the first time in my life, I feel a degree of hope for a more equitable and egalitarian future.

President Trump describes the Black Lives Matter movement as 'a symbol of hate'. The virus starts surging again in many parts of the country. Trump continues to refuse to wear a mask. He holds a rally in Tulsa, Oklahoma. He predicts the arena that seats 19000 will be packed. Just 6200 people turn up, almost all of them maskless. A second outdoor venue has so few people that Trump and his sidekick, Vice President Pence, both cancel appearances there.

Arriving back in Washington, DC, Trump looks deflated and depressed. His shoulders drooped, his tie is undone and hung limply around his neck. The next day he is back to himself. Boasting and blaming.

The virus keeps surging. Trump finally wears a mask. At least once.

The protests continue. Trump decides to send federal agents to Portland, Oregon. The agents are from Customs and Border Control. They are reputed to be brutal. And they are.

The Governor of Oregon says, 'This is a democracy, not a dictatorship. We cannot have secret police abducting people in unmarked vehicles.'

Speaker of the House, Nancy Pelosi, tweets 'Trump and his stormtroopers must be stopped.' Some of the, mostly peaceful, protesters are severely injured.

Trump threatens to send the Federal agents to other cities.

John Lewis, the 80-year-old civil rights icon and member of Congress who recently died, marched in the Black Lives Matter protests although he was unwell. 'This looks and feels so different. It is so much more massive and all inclusive. There will be no turning back,' he said. So many of us are so hopeful.

I read that one in four Americans aged twenty to thirty-one broke quarantine and shelter orders to have sexual contact with someone in April, when the virus was, then, at its peak. I feel bewildered by this until I remember how badly I wanted a haircut.

Mesmerising

I, unexpectedly, have to have orthopedic surgery. This is not great news. After a slew of X-rays, I had an initial, telemedicine appointment with the highly recommended orthopedic surgeon.

The surgeon told me that some of my bones looked very thin. Why is it always the wrong part of you that looks thin? I also have thin wrists. I would so much rather have thin hips or thin thighs.

The orthopedic surgeon was very helpful, very kind and patiently answered all of my questions. I had a lot of questions – I think it could be a Jewish trait to ask a lot of questions, especially about anything medical.

There was, however, a problem. I wasn't bothered by the fact that the orthopedic surgeon looked very young. Every doctor, dentist, podiatrist or physical therapist that I see is young. More than half the world is young. The problem was that the orthopedic surgeon was disconcertingly good-looking. His face filled the screen. I was looking at his very blue eyes, thick, dark hair and perfectly symmetrical facial structure for thirty minutes when I should have been solidly focused on my thin bones.

In an email to the surgeon's medical assistant about the X-ray I had recently had, I mentioned that not only did the surgeon look young, he was also very good-looking.

She replied saying that my email had made her laugh. 'Everyone says that he looks young,' she said.

I don't think she was laughing about my reference to the surgeon's youthful appearance. I think that people assume that if you are female and over seventy you are oblivious to men's good looks. No-one would blink if a 99-year-old man wearing an oxygen mask mentioned a good-looking woman.

'My surgeon is *so* good-looking,' I said to my younger daughter. She started laughing even though I had just told her about my thin bones and the fact that I had to have surgery.

My husband overheard me telling a close friend that Dr X was mesmerisingly good-looking. My husband began teasing me, relentlessly, by repeating the phrase 'mesmerisingly good-looking'. It made me laugh.

The hospital sent me twenty pages of information about the surgery, the post-surgery and the possible side effects and consequences. I found the information quite terrifying. Why do they have to give you so many worrying details, including the worst-case scenario? I am already a worst-case scenario expert. I don't need to increase this expertise.

Six of those disturbing pages were instructions and diagrams for post-surgery. I am not good at interpreting diagrams. I have, more often than I like to acknowledge, been unable to work out how to open a box of cereal or the spout that comes with a container of salt without destroying whatever packaging I am trying to open. I am also not good at following certain instructions, like how to dance, or cross-country ski, or swim anything other than breaststroke.

The first of the post-surgery instructions was how to get into a car after your discharge from hospital. Those instructions were incomprehensible, to me. I didn't even bother trying to understand how to get out of the car, or how to get in and out of bed. I gave those pages to my husband.

I am hoping that the surgeon's mesmerisingly good looks will distract me from the pain and my anxiety, I wrote in an email to a friend.

I realise that I have now mentioned the words 'looks' and 'good-looking' six or seven times. I decide that some things are worth repeating. I am, after all, talking about medical issues.

A friend sends me a link to a series of fascinating documentaries to watch while I am recuperating. The prospect of watching them eases my anxiety. I hope I won't still be trying to get into the car.

The Election

It is Election Day. Everyone I know is in a state of acute anxiety.

I filled out my very simple ballot form very slowly. I was terrified I would make a mistake. You would have thought I was filling out a form about nuclear or quantum physics.

A reassuring sign over the last few days is that Trump has kept lying. He hasn't, at the last minute, turned into Pope Francis or Mother Teresa. Trump lies in the same way that other people breathe.

For two weeks, I have scrutinised the faces of the long lines of people waiting for hours to cast their in-person votes. I have tried to discern whether they are Republicans or Democrats. But the people in these seemingly endless lines are studiously not signalling their political preference. There is not even a hint of the passion, rage or outrage that has propelled a record hundred million people to vote before Election Day.

I am watching CNN. The election results haven't even started to come in and I am on edge. Very on edge. The first results come in. Trump has a very slight lead in Florida. I scramble to find a valium. I don't scramble at my usual speed as I have just had hip surgery. I find the valium and break a five-milligram tablet in half.

Less than an hour later Trump's numbers are rising. I take the other half of the valium. I sit glued to the screen, which is full of numbers – none of which are looking good. I forget about my hip pain and the fact that my swollen hip is five kilometres wider than it was before the surgery.

Trump is now leading in so many parts of the country. I feel distraught. I feel too distraught to feel depressed. My tension level feels unbearable. I have to go to bed. I don't even pause to look in the mirror and see if my hip has managed to ditch even half a kilometre.

The next morning, a New York friend calls to ask if I have any anti-anxiety medication. I tell her I can spare two valium. She says she will pick them up in the afternoon. I feel like a drug dealer. I think that hundreds of thousands – if not millions – of Americans are calling their psychiatrists or general practitioners for anti-anxiety medication or antidepressants.

My husband, who is not easily unnerved, is checking the voting pattern of each state that hasn't yet finished their vote count. He is checking this every ten minutes.

It is now two days after election night. My nerves are shot. My supply of valium has run out. I am shocked by the millions of Americans who have voted for Trump. They obviously love his blatant lies. And they love the hatred that spews out every time he opens his mouth. I find that thought frightening, if not terrifying.

Trump has been talking non-stop. He is talking incessantly about election fraud. I can't bear to hear the sound of his voice. Or his almost predictable vocabulary. Some favorites are dumb, dope, phony, scary, weak, wacky, nasty, terrible, disgraced, racist, fake, overrated.

The *Washington Post* found thirty-two regular Trump insults that he used 1,693 times on 245 targets. And these numbers applied only to his Twitter posts.

I have to try to stop thinking about Trump; I decide to have a shower. Having a shower is no mean feat when you have recently had hip surgery, and that is without taking into account that I now have to include the enlarged dimensions of my hips and thighs. The doctors told me to expect swelling but no-one mentioned five extra kilometres of hips and thighs.

I go into the bathroom. One of my upstairs neighbours is on the phone. I can only hear her when I am in my bathroom. She is often on the phone. I think she must have a lot of friends. I know that she doesn't live alone as I often hear her call out to someone else. Lately she has been talking late at night.

I don't understand the physics of why I can hear her from my bathroom. Our building is substantial and has thick walls. I think it has something to do with a hot-water pipe that runs vertically through the bathroom. I don't know this neighbour. I don't know which apartment she lives in, but I am very fond of her. I also admire her ability to talk on the the phone for hours at a time.

I can't understand every word she says but I can feel the intensity of her intonation. I decide not to have a shower. My neighbour's voice has taken Trump's noise out of my head. Because of the hip surgery I have a new raised toilet. It has padded arms and a padded seat. It is as comfortable as an armchair. I sit down and listen to my neighbour.

Biden is now gaining ground. We all start to feel hopeful. Biden has won several key states and is now ahead in Pennsylvania. Joe Biden and Kamala Harris are looking calm and patient. Many of the rest of us are on the edge of our seats and on the verge of a nervous breakdown.

Suddenly we hear people cheering and whistling and clapping in the street, car horns tooting.

'Biden has won Pennsylvania,' my husband screams out to me. This means Biden has won the election.

I start crying. Out in the street, people are jumping for joy, a young woman is sobbing, someone keeps saying, 'My God, oh my God'.

We are all in a state of disbelief and relief. The sounds of joy and elation feel as though they are filling New York City. And they are. Our elder daughter, who lives in Harlem, sends us a text saying 'Harlem is on fire'. She and her two sons are out in the streets masked and socially distanced, cheering and dancing. It is Saturday November 7th.

There are celebrations all over the country. You can feel the relief and the elation. After a few days, I can feel my own tension diminishing. My fear that Trump will somehow manage to sabotage the election results is evaporating. I start to feel elated.

Trump is stony-faced and grim. He talks nonstop about voter fraud. The word 'fraud' starts sounding like the repetitive refrain of a very bad opera.

For the last two or three days, Trump has been silent. We haven't heard from him. The press says he is fuming. It is clear that we have a president who has locked himself in his bedroom and is smashing his toys.

I decide that even if my hips and thighs decide to reside miles from the rest of me, it won't be the end of the world. Trump will be out shopping for new toys and I will be wearing very roomy kaftans.

My Father

The day my father died was like many other days of his life. He got up early. He ate all of his breakfast. A couple of hours later, he had his morning tea – a cup of tea with milk and sugar, and two or three biscuits.

He had a large, hearty lunch and an extra slice of cake with his afternoon tea. He was in a good mood and looked well. He was almost always in a good mood.

After dinner he had a cup of coffee with milk and sugar and a third of a block of dark, Lindt chocolate as he did every night. At seven-thirty p.m., he went to bed. An hour or so later, he quietly died. He was four months short of his 102nd birthday.

'How are you, darling?' he'd said when he saw me that morning.

I answered him in Polish. '*Bardzo dobrze się mam, dziękuję. Idę do toalety,*' I said. This translates more or less as 'I am good, thank you very much. I am going to the toilet'.

My father started laughing. He wasn't laughing because he thought I was going to the toilet. He was laughing because he knew I was using all eight of the ten words I know in Polish.

When he stopped laughing, he corrected my pronunciation. My father's pronunciation was a whole subject in itself. His Polish accent was, I was told more than once, perfect with an old-fashioned grace. His English wasn't quite as good and did lack a degree of grace.

He called President Trump, President *Tramp*. I explained to him dozens of times that it was 'Trump' not 'Tramp'. 'Yes, President *Tramp*, that is what I did say.' This was his standard answer. I don't know why I was so adamant about Trump not Tramp.

A woman walked by when my father and I were having a Trump versus Tramp conversation. 'He is right,' she said. 'President *Tramp* is a perfect name.' My father beamed. I never corrected Tramp again. I did however strive to change his pronunciation of a few more words.

My father loved his fax machine. He also loved his laptop and his microwave. He would heat up food and clap with joy when the food came out hot. The only problem with the fax machine was that my father called it a 'fux' machine. No matter how many times I told him it was a *fax* machine not a *fux* machine, he couldn't hear the difference.

'I fuxed him yesterday,' he said to me when we were walking along Sixth Avenue. Quite a few people turned their heads. When I walked him to the Broadway-Lafayette St Subway Station where he caught the F Train to his apartment on the Lower East Side, he would wave goodbye to me and sometimes call out, 'I will fux you later.' I learned not to squirm or scurry off. There didn't seem to be any rules in my father's mispronunciations. Fax became fux but Trump became Tramp.

The laptop my father loved could also drive him crazy. He would call my younger daughter at work and say, in a tone that suggested an emergency, 'Darling, my computer is bong.' My daughter, before trying to help him with his laptop, would try to explain to him that he meant *bung*, not bong.

Few Americans would have any idea of what 'bung' means. What does 'bung' mean, anyway? I looked it up. I discovered that, according to *The Farlex Idioms & Slang Dictionary*, it is primarily used in Australia and New Zealand and means die, fail or fall apart, especially financially.

My father's pronunciation was contagious. When my son was two I drove past a house with smoke coming out of its chimney. 'Look, mok, mok,' my son said, pointing to the smoke.

'It's smok not mok,' I said, before realising that my own pronunciation had gone astray.

My father laughed more easily than anyone I have ever known. He laughed so hard that I often thought he was in danger of having a heart attack or a stroke. He found humour in situations that others might find frustrating or irritating.

My father was the light of my childhood. I loved my mother very much but, in a community where everyone was in a state of grief, it was my father who showed me that it was possible to pierce that grief with laughter.

He was loved by so many people. My high-school friends adored him. People he met only once always remembered him. He loved cafes. The staff at Caffe Dante, on MacDougal Street, started preparing his hot chocolate the moment they saw him. They also gave him extra-large helpings of the chocolate gelato he liked to have after his hot chocolate. He was a very lovable man.

He could also be very stubborn. There is a father figure in several of my novels. He is mostly called Edek. My father believed that Edek was him. He was convinced he was Edek. Even when I pointed out so many of the different things that Edek had done – for example, Edek had opened a very successful meatball restaurant on the Lower East Side and Edek, late in his life, had married a blonde, very big-busted Polish woman – my father insisted that he was Edek.

There are parts of my novels that are based on my life

and my father's life. There was quite a lot of Edek in my father. Edek was always generous and always kind. He was mischievous and he was a great dancer. I understand that seeing so much of yourself in a character could lead to some confusion and possibly allow you to think you had opened a meatball restaurant with a blonde, very big-busted attractive Polish woman.

Months later my father conceded that maybe he wasn't one hundred per cent Edek.

One day my father was talking about his very stern father and how he dominated his wife, my father's mother. I had heard quite a lot about my father's father, who was a very successful businessman. I suggested that maybe my father should try to write a memoir.

He thought about it for a few minutes and then said he would write a memoir.

'Do you think it will be published?' he asked me.

'It could be,' I said.

The first two lines of my father's memoir almost sounded like a beginning and an end. He had written, '*I am 87 years old born on 6 July 1916. I lost my wife on 24 August 1986.*' The loss of my mother broke my father's heart.

My father started writing his memoir on a Tuesday. On Friday, he called me to let me know he had finished. I spent a long time trying to explain to him that he had to expand everything he had written and include everything he had left out. Three weeks later he had written twelve pages and was very pleased with himself.

Twelve pages after the date of his birth he had skipped to the fact that he had lived in Australia for over forty years and was now living in New York and he was very happy. He spent another few weeks working on the memoir. He ended it with a large and firm statement. '*The End.*'

My father and I were talking about nothing in particular when he looked at me and said, 'You are my mother and my daughter.' It took me a minute or two to absorb what he had said. And then I wanted to cry at what that short sentence implied.

Almost three years after my father's death, I plucked up the courage to open a file of letters and faxes my father had, over the years, sent to me. In almost every one of my father's letters, he tells me how much he loves me. I think I took those words for granted. Now the same words seem neon-lit. I have always known my father loved me and he knew I loved him, but I wish I had paused and thought more about the unwavering depth of that love.

In a letter to the whole family he begins with '*Dear Lil, David, Paris, Jessica and Gypsy*' and ends with '*I love you all, and this can never change.*'

I had been preparing myself for my father's death for several years. Every time my phone rang late at night I took a deep breath and girded myself for the news. As part of my preparation, I rang the funeral parlour to make sure that all the arrangements were in place. They were bewildered. It turned out that no-one had ever called before the demise of the deceased.

Sometime around my father's 98th birthday I had somehow lulled myself into feeling that my father would always be there. He had, in his nineties, survived several bouts of the flu, stomach viruses and other illnesses. He recovered from all of these with lightning speed. He was knocked over by a reasonably large van while he was crossing Essex Street. He got up and then argued with the paramedics when they wanted to take him to hospital.

When my father died, I felt utterly shocked. I felt distraught. I couldn't believe he was dead. I called my children. I knew that they would feel very distressed.

At the funeral parlour I had to identify the body. I didn't expect this. Jews, on the whole, don't view the body. I was frightened – no, terrified – of seeing my father dead. When I finally took the elevator to go to the chapel or, as it is sometimes called, 'the visiting room', I was shocked, again. My father looked just like himself. And, he looked well. He didn't look dead.

I started stroking his head and crying and kissing him. 'I am so sorry, I am so sorry, I am so sorry,' I said, over and over again. I didn't know what I was saying sorry for. I think I was telling him how sorry I was that he had died.

My husband and I were both crying when we left the funeral parlour, although I felt much better after I had seen my father and been able to kiss him and talk to him.

At home, I wrote a list of things I had to do. At the top of the list was finding a rabbi who would not mention the word 'God'. My father was adamant that there was no God. He was not the only survivor of Nazi death camps who lost all faith in God. The rabbi we chose understood.

We had a small family funeral. There were ten of us and two of my father's eight great-grandchildren. My son wanted to see my father one last time. The driver of the hearse arrived. I asked him about seeing my father. He hesitated and then nodded his head.

The hearse was parked in the cemetery's relatively crowded car park. We each took our turn to say goodbye and give him one last kiss. My father would have loved the fact that he was last seen in an open casket that was sticking out of the back of a hearse, in a car park. We were all crying as we walked behind the hearse to my father's burial plot.

The gravesite was marked with my father's name and a Star of David. We each spoke at the service. I can't remember a word I said. What was crystal clear was how much each of us loved him. I threw the first shovelful of earth onto his coffin and then suddenly became very anxious about how on earth my father was going to be able to breathe with all that earth on top of him.

Only in New York

*New York is a walker's city. You can walk for hours. The streets
slip by. There is so much to look at, so much to take in.
I walk a lot. Especially when I am not writing ...*

Lily Brett's love affair with New York began as an outsider in her
late teens when she was posted on assignment there as a young
Australian rock journalist. In her early forties she returned,
together with her soul mate and three children, to start a new life,
and for more than three decades she has called New York home.

This witty, candid and moving collection of short pieces
celebrates the city that's now part of her heartbeat. A compulsive
walker, Brett takes us to her favourite places and introduces us
to the characters of the city that has nurtured, perplexed and
inspired her. She brings to life the delights of Chinatown, the
majesty of Grand Central Station, the lure of spandex and
sequins in the Garment District, and the peculiarity of canine
couture. And she muses on the miracle of love in the Lodz
ghetto, the possibility of loneliness amidst skyscrapers, and the
joy and redemption in a child's curiosity.

Full of wisdom, humour and grace, *Only in New York* is a
human portrait of a city much loved – and of a woman in step
with herself.

'Pithy, entertaining and personal.' *Weekend Australian*

'New York is a city of character and characters and anyone
thinking of visiting should use this as a guide to its flavour.'
Herald Sun

'Charm[ing] ... Her snippets are short and sharp as they portray
the essence of New York.' *West Australian*

Lola Bensky

Winner of the Prix Médicis Étranger

Lola Bensky is a nineteen-year-old rock journalist who irons her hair straight and asks a lot of questions. A high-school dropout, she's not sure how she got the job – but she's been sent by her Australian newspaper right to the heart of the London music scene at the most exciting time in music history: 1967.

In London, New York and LA, Lola interviews the biggest rock stars of the day, including Jimi Hendrix, Mick Jagger and Janis Joplin. But she begins to wonder whether the questions she asks are really a substitute for questions about her parents' past that can't be asked or answered. With time, she discovers the question of what it means to be human is the hardest one for anyone – including herself – to answer.

Drawing on her own experiences as a young journalist, Lily Brett shows in *Lola Bensky* just why she is one of our most distinctive and internationally acclaimed authors.

'Brett has created in Lola a typically winning character: curious, self-conscious, naive and neurotic, a wary Jewish girl locked in trench warfare with her waistline.' *The Age*

'Funny, warm and insightful.' *Herald Sun*

'A book that will entertain legions of readers.' *Courier Mail*

Too Many Men

Winner of the Commonwealth Writers' Prize

Ruth Rothwax, a successful woman with her own business, Rothwax Correspondence, can find order and meaning in writing words for other people – condolence letters, thank-you letters, even you-were-great-in-bed letters. But as the daughter of Edek Rothwax, an Auschwitz survivor with a somewhat idiosyncratic approach to the English language, Ruth can find no words to understand the loss her family experienced during World War II.

Ruth is obsessed with the idea of returning to Poland with her father, but she doesn't quite understand why she feels this so intensely. To make sense of her family's past, yes. To visit the places where her beloved mother and father lived and almost died, certainly. But she knows there's more to this trip. By facing Poland, and the past, she can finally confront her own future.

'One of a rare breed . . . a polished stylist with brains, wit, and a message.' *Sun Herald*

'*Too Many Men* is [Lily Brett's] masterpiece.' *The Australian*

'This is writing of a high order of accomplishment.' *Sydney Morning Herald*

'A very funny writer with a feel for the vagaries of conversation and behaviour.' *The Age*